THE NEW FEMALE
CRIMINAL

THE NEW FEMALE CRIMINAL

Empirical Reality or Social Myth?

JoAnn Gennaro Gora

PRAEGER

PRAEGER SPECIAL STUDIES • PRAEGER SCIENTIFIC

Library of Congress Cataloging in Publication Data

Gora, JoAnn Gennaro.
    The new female criminal.

    Bibliography: p.
    Includes index.
    1. Female offenders—New Jersey—Longitudinal
studies. I. Title.
HV6046.G66   1982   364.3'74'09749   82-7685
ISBN 0-03-062007-4   AACR2

Published in 1982 by Praeger Publishers
CBS Educational and Professional Publishing
a Division of CBS Inc.
521 Fifth Avenue, New York, New York 10175 U.S.A.

123456789   052   987654321

Printed in the United States of America

To Jesse Dylan,

for he loves a good story well told,

and to Eleanore and Vincent Gennaro,

for always caring

ACKNOWLEDGMENTS

The research process is exciting but not necessarily pleasant. There are too many people in whose interest it is not to cooperate. Practically no one sees love of truth or advancing the state of knowledge as sufficient reason to cooperate. Consequently, ardent researchers (and these are the only ones who succeed) must use a variety of skills and tactics to gain access to the necessary data. In this case the data source was police records. Police departments have never thought of sociologists or researchers as natural allies. Too often the debunking nature of sociological research has resulted in alienating the layman who initially cooperated. This is not, however, the place to document the sociology of criminological data collection. Suffice it to say in this research, that for every one police chief who cooperated there were a dozen who did not. In the end, I was incredibly grateful to the open-minded, forthright police chief who said "yes" and to the criminal justice planning agency that helped with that initial contact. The county probation department chief that I contacted was a unique and rare combination of integrity and scholarly disposition. He opened his department's files to me without hesitation. Perhaps the most important group of people I came to know were the police officers who actually accepted my presence, were honestly friendly and helpful in explaining how the files had been set up, and, in the end, mucked around with me in dirty basements and musty closets to find old rap sheets and ancient police reports that I insisted were vital. These police officers were smart, kind, and gave me insight into police work that I lacked. This study would not have been possible without the understanding, cooperation, support, and enthusiasm of these people. They made the months of data collection interesting, enjoyable, and educational. I wish I could name them all here.

The idea for this research was my own. I gained access to police records as a result of my own footwork, and there was no foundation or government grant to ease the way. However, there were friends and mentors whose intelligence and insight were truly invaluable and whom I came to depend upon for guidance. At Rutgers University, I am most indebted to Richard Stephenson, Allan Horwitz, Steven Casey, Paul Lerman, Lynda Glennon, Harry Bredemier, and Matilda Riley, from whose encouragement and critical analyses I profited greatly. In addition I am grateful to Fairleigh Dickinson University for granting me a leave of absence during which the final analysis and writing were completed.

vii

I have been fortunate to have had the opportunity to exchange ideas with many thoughtful people. Without the friendships of Irene Thomson, Joe Curran, Beth Bogan, Kenneth Greene, Jeff Clark, and Robert Greenfield, I would have missed out on many hours of conversation that enriched my thinking and my life. I am especially thankful to have worked with Marlene Falk, who is a unique combination of warmth, competence, and intelligence.

Finally, I want to thank Ted Gora and Gloria Nemerowicz, who have given me years of emotional support, enthusiasm, needed advice, and encouragement.

CONTENTS

LIST OF TABLES

LIST OF FIGURES

THE NEW FEMALE
CRIMINAL

1

THEORETICAL AND ANALYTICAL FRAMEWORK

INTRODUCTION

The volume of theoretical and empirical literature on female criminality is but a small fraction of that on crime and delinquency among males. This fact is commonly attributed to two causes: there are fewer female criminals than male criminals (Sutherland and Cressey 1970, p. 126), and female offenses are considered "criminologically much less interesting" (Cowie, Cowie, and Slater 1968, p.1), that is, offenses committed by women are not as violent or as varied as those committed by men.

However, within the last 15 years, the Uniform Crime Reports (UCR) of the Federal Bureau of Investigation indicate that the arrest rate of women has soared and the type of crime committed by women has become more serious. How should these events be interpreted? Do these events lend credibility to a specific theory of crime causation?

A review of the theoretical literature shows that female and male crimes have been explained quite differently. That is, the factors that are thought to explain male crime have not been applied to female criminal activity. There have been two major schools of thought attempting to explain the etiology of female crime. The earlier, traditional school of thought, represented by the writings of Lombroso (1920), Pollak (1950), Thomas (1907; 1923), Cowie, Cowie, and Slater (1968), Konopka (1966), and Vedder and Somerville (1970) emphasizes the psychological and physiological factors inherent in "the nature of women" as motivating criminal behavior. Recently, a second school of thought has developed. These theorists have postulated the importance of social and cultural factors (especially sex role socialization) in explaining the existence (or lack) of female crime (Adler 1975; David 1972; Hoffman-Bustamante 1973; Nye 1958; Simon 1975; Toby 1957).

1

The traditional theorists, who emphasized the physiological and psychological aspects of female offenders, seemingly tried to answer the question, What disposes women, who are by nature gentle, passive, narcissistic, and dependent, to commit crimes? The more recent work in the field, which has emphasized social and cultural rather than sexual factors, seems to be posing the questions: Why have women not committed more crimes? and What has held them back?

The recent rise in the arrest rate of women has been interpreted as evidence bearing on the credibility of the nontraditional theories. That is, some sociologists have attributed the rise in arrests to a change in female criminal behavior reflective of the change in sex role definitions brought on by recent social movements (Adler 1975; David 1972; Simon 1975). Therefore, women are more criminalistic today because they are responding to changes in opportunities to commit crime and a changing self-image. This research probes that hypothesis. Simply, does the rise in arrest rates indicate that women are responding to a change in sex role definition? Is the rise in arrest rates empirical data that lends credibility to the sociocultural theories of female crime causation?

This chapter will explore the theoretical literature on female crime causation and suggest a research design that will more adequately probe the hypothesis that the rise in female arrests is due to an increase in female criminal activity brought on by changing sex role definitions of behavior.

A REVIEW OF THE THEORETICAL LITERATURE

Introduction

Theories attempting to explain male crime have largely focused on the importance of social and cultural factors (Cloward and Ohlin 1960, 1970; Cohen 1955; Hirschi 1969; Merton 1938, 1957; Miller 1958; Sutherland and Cressey 1970). Social-structural factors such as social class position, anomie, access to legitimate and illegitimate opportunities, and subcultural factors have been explored. Yet, theorists who have studied the etiology of female criminality have, in the main, emphasized the physiological or psychological aspects inherent in the "nature of women." Female criminal activity is usually understood as an activity of individuals, with little attention paid to the social and cultural factors that may be significant. The first theorists described female criminality as a product of biological abnormalities (Glueck 1934; Lombroso 1920). Subsequently, psychological theories were formulated that were based on earlier assumptions of universal physiological traits of women. Thus, Freud's (1933) assumptions about women's reproductive instinct, innate passivity, narcissism, and deceitfulness provided the foundation for the works of Pollak (1950), Konopka (1966), and Vedder and Somerville (1970). Female deviance, then, became a product of sexual maladjustment and neurosis.

Competing with this long-standing view of the etiology of female crime is the recent work of several sex role theorists* who have emphasized the impact of sociocultural factors (specifically, socialization and sex role learning in the family) in regulating the quantity and quality of female crime. These later theorists rejected what they perceived to be "the sexist, racist and classist" foundations of earlier theories (Klein 1973, p. 6).

In this chapter these two schools of thought will be reviewed and probed for competing hypotheses.

Theories Emphasizing Physiological or
Psychological Factors

Beginning with the turn-of-the-century writer Cesare Lombroso, a handful of criminologists have been concerned with the etiology of female crime. To varying degrees, their theories of criminality are based on "implicit assumptions about the physiological and psychological nature of women that are explicit in Lombroso's work" (Klein 1973, p. 7).

Lombroso stresses the argument that individuals develop differentially within sexual and racial limitations that differ hierarchically from the most highly developed, the white man, to the most primitive, the nonwhite woman. He traces a general pattern of evolution that explains variations in the development of groups. Thus, "even the female criminal is monotonous and uniform compared with her male companion, just as, in general, woman is inferior to man" (Lombroso 1920, p. 122). This is due to her being "atavistically nearer to her origin than the male" (p. 107). Lombroso develops a biological explanation of male and female crime, introducing the notion of the "born criminal" (p. 99). Comparing convicted criminals with noncriminals, he theorizes that certain physical characteristics mark one as being atavistic. These "primitive traits" (dark hair, moles, obesity) are signs of a criminal disposition.

Within a framework emphasizing the biological limits of woman's nature, the female offender is defined as "masculine." The normal

---

*"Sex role theorists" is the label I have applied to the work of Hoffman-Bustamante (1973), Simon (1975), and Adler (1975).

woman is "feminine." Characteristics of the skull, physiognomy, and brain capacity of female criminals are described as similar to those of of the man, normal or criminal. According to Lombroso, the female offender often has a "virile cranium and body hair" (1920, p. 76). Lombroso also enumerates female psychological traits that contribute to criminality. Women commit crime because they are insensitive to pain and lack moral refinement.

> Women have many traits in common with children: their moral sense is deficient, they are revengeful and jeal-ous. . . . In ordinary cases these defects are neutralized by piety, maternity, want of passion, sexual coldness, weakness and an undeveloped intelligence. [1920, p. 152]

W. I. Thomas builds on Lombroso's biological scheme, em-phasizing the importance of the physical differences between the sexes. In Sex and Society (1907) he notes the following:

> What we look for most in the female is feminity, and when we find the opposite in her, we must conclude as a rule that there must be some anomaly. . . . In the portraits of Red Indian and Negro beauties, whom it is difficult to recognize for women, so huge are their jaws and cheekbones, so hard and coarse their features, and the same is often the case in their crania and brains. [1907, p. 112]

In The Unadjusted Girl (1923) Thomas moves from an exclusively physiological focus and deals with female criminality as a "normal" response under certain social conditions. The importance of social controls in directing an individual's basic drives, or "wishes" as Thomas calls them, is stressed. It is "the definition of the situation" that controls behavior, and socialization, not punishment, that regu-lates action. However, the "nature of women" and the motivation for crime remains essentially unchanged; delinquent girls are motivated by the desire for excitement. Thomas feels that

> the beginning of delinquency in girls is usually an impulse to get amusement, adventure, pretty clothes, favorable notice, distinction and freedom in the larger world. [1923, p. 109]

Economic factors in delinquency are ignored and the female criminal emerges as an "adventuress."

An unattached woman has a tendency to become an adventuress not so much on economic as on psychological
grounds. Life is rarely so hard that a young woman cannot earn her bread; but she cannot always live and have
the stimulation she craves. [1923, p. 241]

Freud is remembered because he defined the healthy feminine
psyche for future theorists. Psychological characteristics such as
masochism, narcissism, passivity, and sexual indifference were defined as anatomically based, universal feminine traits. Historical
possibilities of change in social or sexual roles are overlooked because of the explicit biological tenets of the theory. Thus Freud (1933)
laid the groundwork for future theorists' attempts to relate psychological traits to biological characteristics.

Otto Pollak's treatise The Criminality of Women (1950) has been
called "the major work in the field of women and crime in the postwar years" (Klein 1973, p. 21). Pollak insists on the importance of
biological and psychological factors acting in concert in accounting
for female criminality and in explaining low official arrest rates for
women.

Menstruation, pregnancy and menopause have to be considered of central research interest . . . the student of
female criminality cannot afford to overlook the generally known and recognized fact that these generative
phases are frequently accompanied by psychological dis-
turbances which may upset the need and satisfaction
balance of the individual or weaken her internal inhibi-
tions and thus become causative factors in female
crime. [1950, p. 157]

Pollak lists the psychological consequences of the biological
life-cycle phases. Menstruation, as a symbol of womanhood, arouses
feelings of irritation and protest against the demeaned status of women
in society. Pregnancy is a source of "irritation, anxiety and emotional upheaval" (1950, p. 158). "Menopause is a threat to a woman's
general marital existence" (1950, p. 158). At all times the "distur-
bance of the emotional balance of the individual promotes criminal
activity" (1950, p. 159).

Pollak also notes the influence on criminality of three social
factors: the double standard of sexual morality, modern advertising
techniques, and the use of females as domestics. The double standard of sexual morality acts as an irritant to women, arousing their
desire for revenge. Modern sales promotion techniques stimulate

consumer greed. The female as domestic is stimulated to criminal
activity by the frustration of relative deprivation. With these as
incentives, the modern woman, according to Pollak, uses traditional
cultural roles as opportunities for the commission of crime. As
mother and wife, she commits crimes against the person (murder
and manslaughter). As consumer or worker, she commits crimes
against property (for example, theft) (1950, p. 163).

Pollak concludes that "the amount of female crime has been
greatly underestimated by traditional opinion" (1950, p. 16). He postulates the existence of large amounts of "hidden crime," because
women are protected from prosecution by chivalry and from detection
by deceit and concealment. In support of his belief in women's ability
to deceive and conceal, he notes that women can feign emotion during
sexual intercourse and conceal their time of menstruation.

> Our sex mores force women to conceal every four weeks
> the period of menstruation. . . . They thus make con-
> cealment and misrepresentation in the eyes of women
> socially required and must condition them to a different
> attitude toward veracity than men. [1950, p. 11]

Cowie, Cowie, and Slater (1968), studying a group of girls re-
siding at a training school, note many environmental factors (disturbed
family life, poor education, economic poverty) that correlate highly
with delinquency. The influence of social factors in crime causation
is recognized, but is considered more important in the study of male
offenders (1968, p. 175). The authors feel strongly that the difference
in delinquency rate and type of delinquency committed by boys and
girls is closely connected to

> the masculine or feminine pattern of development of
> personality [which is] related to biological and somatic
> differences, including differences in hormonal balance
> and these would at the ultimate remove be derived from
> chromosomal differences between the sexes. [1968,
> p. 170]

The physiological differences between the female offender and the
nonoffender are stressed: "Delinquents tend to be larger than controls
and overgrown and to have markedly masculine traits" (pp. 171-72).
The authors equate masculinity and feminity—social categories—with
maleness and femaleness—physical categories. With this perspective, the female offender is defined as "masculine," since she exhib-
its the "energy, aggressiveness, enterprise and rebelliousness to

break through conformist habits" (1968, p. 171). In their view, a female is feminine, that is, weak, dependent, narcissistic. Therefore, the criminal must be a product of defective heredity or a genetic anomaly. One of the hypotheses developed is "the greater the degree of masculinity, the greater the delinquent predisposition" (1968, p. 171). Their thesis is that male–female constitutional (somatic, especially hormonal) differences lie at the root of sexual differences in delinquency rates. They assert that "sex chromosome constitution is one of the basic factors determining the liability to delinquency" (1968, p. 172).

Vedder and Somerville (1970) emphasize the importance of individual and family pathologies. As therapy, they recommend measures to strengthen the family, noting, however, that

> special attention should be given to girls, taking into consideration their constitutional, biological and psychological differences. [1970, p. 153]

They do not state what the biological or constitutional differences are but the psychological problems are noted.

> The female offender's goal, as any woman's is a happy and successful marriage; therefore, her self image is dependent upon the establishment of satisfactory relations with the opposite sex. [1970, p. 153]

In analyzing the disproportionate number of black girls in their sample of incarcerated offenders, they reduce economic and social factors to the problem of developing "healthy, feminine narcissism."

> The conflict and frustrations of the normal adolescent are compounded . . . for the delinquent Negro girl. . . . The black girl is, in fact, the antithesis of American beauty. However loved she may be by her mother, family and community, she has no real basis of feminine attractiveness on which to build a sound feminine narcissism. When to her physical unattractiveness is added discouraging, deprecating mother-family-community environment, there is a damaged self concept and an impairment of her feminine narcissism which will have profound consequences for her character development. [1970, p. 159]

Gisela Konopka's study of several hundred adolescent, delinquent girls in institutions in Minnesota (1966) also contains assumptions about the psychological and physiological nature of women. She postulates that the girls' delinquency is a result of loneliness, fear and distrust of adults, poor self-image, and a lack of communication with others. She emphasizes, "What I found in the girl in conflict was . . . loneliness accompanied by despair" (1966, p. 140). She notes that boys do not have as severe a sense of isolation as girls. She distinguishes the sexes on emotional grounds.

> While these girls also strive for independence, their
> need for dependence is unusually great. . . . The de-
> linquent girl suffers, like most boys, from a lack of
> success, lack of opportunity, but her drive for success
> is never separated from her need for people, for inter-
> personal involvement. [1966, p. 40-41]

In analyzing the roots of loneliness experienced by her respondents, she employs a Freudian perspective, citing menstruation as a significant event in a girl's development.

While it is generally recognized that a broken home or a poor home life is related to delinquency among boys, this is felt to be even more crucial in the case of girls. Again, the interpretation of this variable is much more psychological or personal than sociological (Barker and Adams 1962; Cowie, Cowie, and Slater 1968; Denys 1969; Gilbert 1972; Konopka 1966; Morris 1964; Pollak and Friedman 1969; Riege 1972). Barker and Adams (1962) propose that many of the females' delinquent acts are psychological reaction formations against absent or inadequate fathers. Morris (1964) stressed the higher incidence of family tensions within the broken home. Gilbert (1972) found that good discipline from the mother was a factor militating against delinquency in lower-class girls. Riege (1972) found loneliness and low self-esteem to characterize delinquent more than nondelinquent girls. Denys (1969) cites the importance of feelings of isolation and insecurity and "subtle rejection by parents" (p. 185). These studies seem to adhere to the idea that delinquency is primarily an adaptation to personal problems.

This literature, then, has emphasized psychological and physiological factors that lead to individual maladjustments and result in delinquent behavior. Female delinquency is seen primarily as an adaptation to personal problems. A few theorists, however, have taken a more sociocultural perspective and have developed a sex role theory of delinquent behavior.

Sex Role Theories

The sex role theorist, in contrast to the proponent of the biological-psychological approach to the explanation of female crime, recognizes the importance of sex role and socialization practices and gives less recognition to biological or constitutional factors in the etiology of female crime.

Ivan Nye's (1958) view is that delinquent behavior is natural; socially conforming behavior is an artificially induced deviation. This deviation is produced through the force of two kinds of controls: internal controls that are the result of early childhood socialization practices, and direct controls that are the prohibitions and punishments leveled by societal institutions. Nye contends that adolescent girls experience a much more restricted life than do boys. Both the family and the wider environment exercise more interest in and more control over their behavior. Therefore, he hypothesizes that girls are less likely to be delinquent because they are supervised more and kept under better control, especially by their families. He suggests that this family control constitutes a kind of bottleneck restraining them from their naturally delinquent path. Any slackening of control that loosens this bottleneck will have an impact on the behavior of the adolescent girl. So it is that he finds in his random sample of school age adolescents in three small Washington towns that while girls commit fewer delinquent acts than boys, family disorganization has a greater impact on their behavior than it does on that of the boys. *
He notes that the behavior of fathers was more often significantly related to delinquency than the behavior of mothers. He hypothesizes that mothers adhere to a consensual standard of parenting, whereas fathers vary in their view of their role as parent and are not guided by a generally accepted standard of conduct. In those families with negligent or absent fathers Nye was most likely to find girls with antisocial behavior. As he would say: family control slackened, the bottleneck loosened, delinquency resulted.

Over twenty years ago, Walter Reckless suggested the importance of role theory in explaining crime statistics. While also noting the importance of other factors such as "companionship, guilt and the psychopathic personality" in explaining crime, he concludes that

> the principal differences between men and women in crime are largely explicable by the roles cast for men and women in our society. . . . The contention herein is that role theory as developed by American Sociologists goes far in accounting for the specifics in male and female criminality. [1957, p. 6]

---

*The importance of family disorganization in delinquency causation has been discussed by Jackson Toby (1957).

Reckless asserted the importance of social roles in explaining behavior but clung to the belief that "the role which men and women play in society (is) a result of their biology, psychology and social position" (1957, p. 8). More recent theorists have rejected the putative biological and psychological basis of sex roles and focused on the sociological aspect of sex roles.

Dale Hoffman-Bustamante (1973) has developed the most complete sex role theory of female crime to date. Using a sociological perspective, she hypothesizes that crimes committed by women are the outcome of five major factors: differential role expectations for men and women, sex differences in socialization patterns and application of social control, structurally determined differences in opportunities to commit particular offenses, differential access to or pressures toward criminally oriented subcultures and careers, and sex differences built into the crime categories themselves (1973, p. 117).

In agreement with Nye, Hoffman-Bustamante argues that the vast difference in arrest rates between males and females is accounted for by differential socialization and differential use of social control.

> Females are more closely supervised and more strictly disciplined in our society. Yet social control in the form of informal sanctions applied by primary and secondary groups is imposed more consistently and for more minor deviations from accepted standards. This results in a situation where females have been taught to conform to more rigid standards and rewarded for such behavior, whereas males are told to conform, yet rewarded for flaunting many conventional standards. [1973, p. 120]

She also notes the influence of the media images of role-appropriate behavior.

> Cultural heroes, such as cowboys, private-eyes, football players, adventurers and two-fisted cops are evidence of the types of models emulated by many boys. Cultural heroes for girls are either non-existent or portrayed as successful suburban housewives and mothers. [1973, p. 120]

Furthermore, sex roles dictate what skills an individual will have for committing crime. For instance, women are given fewer opportunities to learn how to use the weapons necessary for criminal activity than are men. Women, in the course of growing up, usually are not encouraged to learn how to fight or even how to defend themselves. Rather, they are encouraged to think of themselves as weak and vulnerable. Thus, it is not surprising that in the commission of homicide, women more often use household objects in their own home against their own kin or paramour (1973, p. 122). Men are more likely to beat their victims to death or to use a gun, and the crime usually does not take place at the offender's home. Female robbers typically do not use force or weapons and usually act as an accomplice, not an instigator, to the crime (Conklin 1972, p. 103).

According to Sutherland and Cressey, "it is probable that fraud is the most prevalent crime in America" (1970, p. 42). Most fraud is committed by individuals who are owners or managers of large companies or corporations. Women generally are not in positions of authority in business, so that their work is more closely supervised. They do not have the opportunity to commit fraud. Similarly with embezzlement: women steal from charities, or as bank employees shave small amounts off large accounts. Women typically do not have the training or the business position that would permit them to commit fraud or larceny on a large scale.

Noting that the female arrest rate for forgery and counterfeiting exceed their average for all crimes,* Hoffman-Bustamante explains that counterfeiting may fit well into a woman's sphere of responsibility for paying the bills. She has the opportunity, and she may also have the skill and feel the type of economic pressure that compels some individuals to commit crime (1973, p. 128).

Female arrest rates also exceed their expected average for all juvenile crimes for curfew and runaway offenses. This is another example of the influence of sex roles. Girls out alone at night are more likely to be questioned than are boys. Parents are more likely to be concerned with the absence of their "defenseless" daughters than they are about the absence of their "wild" sons. Hoffman-Bustamante notes that

> these two categories illustrate the tendency to treat
> women in a paternalistic manner and express concern
> for their "state of living" or "what they are becoming"
> over and beyond specific offenses they commit. [1973,
> p. 131]

Writing in this decade, Simon (1975) and Adler (1975; 1978) were among the first to attribute the rising crime rate to the impact of the women's movement.

---

*Hoffman-Bustamante computes the average arrest rate for women and calls special attention to those crimes in which the average is exceeded.

Simon conducts an extensive analysis of the <u>Uniform Crime Reports</u> over a ten-year period. She attributes changes in female criminal activity to changes in opportunities to commit crime. Thus, she notes that property crimes have shown the greatest increases; entry into white-collar positions has facilitated the acts of larceny, embezzlement, fraud, forgery, and counterfeiting. Violent offenses have shown the slowest rate of increase.

Freda Adler has utilized unstructured, qualitative interviews with inmates, police officials, and prison administrators to suggest the impact of the women's rights movement on the activity of female offenders. Adler contends that changes in the definition of the female sex role have led to increases in the amount and the seriousness of female criminal activity. Noting that men and women are more alike than different, she asserts that previous criminological patterns were a product of sex roles.

> Their [women's] resort to petty social gambits and petty crimes was a reflection more of their petty strengths than their petty drives. [1975, p. 11]

To the women's movement Adler credits the "changing status of women in the family, marriage, employment and social position" (1975, p. 13). However, liberation has a "darker side." It is this "shady aspect of liberation" that has brought on increased female criminal activity and is a part of the price society must pay for needed social change. She contends that

> in the same way that women are demanding equal opportunity in the fields of legitimate endeavor, a similar number of determined women are forcing their way into the world of major crimes. [1975, p. 13]

While not maintaining that the Mafia is an equal opportunity employer or that the "new criminal" recognizes the social roots of her new aspirations, the causal link between the women's movement and increased criminal involvement is made clear.

> Like her legitimate-based sister, the female criminal knows too much to pretend, or return to her former role as a second-rate criminal confined to "feminine" crimes such as shoplifting and prostitution. She has had a taste of financial victory. In some cases, she has had a taste of blood. Her appetite, however, appears to be only whetted. [1975, p. 15]

Quoting extensively from interviews, she notes that the individual's motivation is neither explicitly ideological nor psychological; rather, it is financial. One interviewee stated the following:

> I needed more money, you know, and I was taking these
> small transistor radios because there was this guy who
> would take all the radios I could give him for five or ten
> dollars each. . . . Then one day it hit me. Wow! It
> was weird. What the hell was I doing just taking radios
> all these months? I was knocking myself out for a bunch
> of five buck radios. . . . I got with a friend . . . and we
> started taking color TV sets! I mean, if I was going to
> rip something off, why the hell didn't I take Cadillacs
> for all that time instead of some goddamned radios?
> [1975, p. 11]

Adler insists that the women's movement has forced girls to become more goal-oriented—"to yield to the necessity, once exclusively male, to make one's way and to prove oneself in the world" (1975, p. 94). With their preliminary training in the student protests of the 1960s, women have a new self-image. From her interviews, she concludes that for the "new" women, "prostitution and shoplifting are not their style: embezzlement, robbery and assault are more congenial to their self image" (1975, p. 27).

Adler's study Sisters in Crime has received marked publicity. Her explanation of the activity of females in terrorist activities has been widely publicized in the popular media (Adler 1978). Yet, Sisters in Crime relies on qualitative data—intensive interviews. It is an exploratory study that can, at best, induce hypotheses; it cannot probe them. Because of the undetermined biases of the nonprobability sampling procedure, this qualitative study cannot adequately test hypotheses. However, from the works of Adler, Simon, and Hoffman-Bustamante, hypotheses can be derived that could be probed. This, of course, is the intent of this research.

ANALYSIS

Introduction

The traditional theories have been criticized because of their emphasis on physiological and psychological attributes that are assumed to be universal and timeless. How can a constant (the "inherent nature of women") explain a variable (the changing arrest rate)? These theorists do not attribute woman's nature to historical, social, or cultural forces, but rather to biological facts that are innate, inherent, and uninfluenced by social change or cultural discontinuities.

Sex role theory is sensitive to the impact of social change. Recognizing social and cultural factors as important influences on the etiology of female crime, it would predict that the female crime rate would be influenced by social movements affecting sex role imagery and socialization practices. The purported large increases in the number of adjudicated females has lent credibility to this theoretical school. This study seeks to examine more closely the increases in the arrest figures and to test sex role theory by using it to predict the distribution or pattern of increases within segments of society.

The Research Design

Primarily, the analysis investigates this question: Has female crime changed over time in (1) quantity or (2) quality? The comparison is always between females and males in one time period or among females (or males) in different time periods.

Quantity

To investigate increases in the extent or number of female arrests, it is necessary to examine the percentage increase over time in the number of females arrested using males as a control group. This will determine whether the rate of increase of female arrests exceeds the rate of increase for males and whether there has been a change over time in this pattern. In addition, change in the number of female arrests must be examined in the light of demographic changes in the crime-prone age groups. Thus, it will be evident that arrests are either keeping pace with demographic changes in the population or that they now include a disproportionate share of the population.

Moreover, it has always been assumed that an increase in the number of arrests is equivalent to an increase in the number of offenders, or individuals arrested. However, it is important to examine police record-keeping procedures to know whether this in fact is true. An increase in number of arrests may not signify an increase in number of individuals arrested, but rather an increase in arrests of a limited number of individuals. For example, a notation of six arrests for obscene telephone calls may mean six arrests of one individual who has made six obscene telephone calls at different times or arrests of six different individuals for making six different obscene telephone calls. It is the latter situation that sex role theorists (and the media) have been proclaiming and that signifies involvement by an increased number of females. Similarly, any changes in record-keeping procedures over time that would inflate the UCR statistics would be important to recognize.

Quality

Sex role theory predicts that social movements for equality will produce (1) a change in the seriousness of crimes committed by females in different historical periods and (2) a change in the racial, age, and social class distribution of female offenders.

To examine patterns in the seriousness of offenses, a cohort analysis is necessary. This analytical tool allows a longitudinal approach that searches for patterns between same-age cohorts born in different historical time periods and, therefore, subject to different socialization influences (intercohort analysis). It also permits comparison of the effects of aging on different cohorts (intracohort analysis). Using a control group of males facilitates the interpretation of changes in the seriousness of female offenses of same-age cohorts (intercohort analysis) or of different cohorts as they age (intracohort analysis).

Sex role theory emphasizes social and cultural factors that influence sex role definitions and socialization practices. It is these changes that predict increasing seriousness of female offenses as social movements effect "role convergence" (Weis 1976) and the loosening of social controls on women. Simon attributes changes in the kinds of crimes committed to increased opportunities in the business world. Adler uses interviews with police officers and female inmates to argue that there has been a change in self-image that necessitates a rejection of "feminine" crimes and a desire to snag a bigger piece of the pie through increased involvement in larcenies, embezzlement, and robbery—the more profitable crimes.

There is a consensus in the literature that female involvement in the past has been restricted to a limited number of specific offenses. Researchers (Clark and Haurek 1966; Cockburn and McClay 1965; Davis 1937; Elliott 1952; Felice and Offord 1971, 1972; Smith 1962) argue that the crimes for which women are arrested and convicted have been much the same for hundreds of years. Other research indicates that the offenses for which females are most likely to be arrested are: incorrigibility (Barker and Adams 1962; Forer 1970; Vedder and Somerville 1970), various sexual offenses (Chesney-Lind 1973; Datesman, Scarpitti, and Stephenson 1975; Vedder 1954; Vedder and Somerville 1970), running away from home (Barker and Adams 1962; Chesney-Lind 1973; Forer 1970; Vedder and Somerville 1970), truancy (Forer 1970; Miller 1973; Vedder and Somerville 1970), and shoplifting (Adler 1975).

Therefore, this study compares the most frequent offenses of males and females across different historical time periods in order to determine the extent of change in the frequency of occurrence of different offenses. Within each sex group, the rank order of the mean frequencies of delinquent involvement will be computed and the rank order correlation coefficients for the two groups will be compared.

If indeed the women's movement has led to an increase in the extent and seriousness of female criminal activity, then the increase in activity should be most noticeable among whites, the middle class, and the young. These are the three groups most likely to have been influenced by changes in sex role definitions and socialization practices. The lower-class, black woman has never been as closely bound by the traditional cultural stereotype of normative female behavior as the middle-class, white woman. Also, it is middle-class, white women and the young who have been most receptive to changing sex role definitions (Hare 1970; LaRue 1970). Adler (1975) states that such activities as student protests and civil rights demonstrations helped to teach women their new roles. Again, this involvement is class-linked and, hence, would not have the same effect on lower-class females. In the past, the female criminal population has been heavily populated by lower-class blacks. If more lower-class blacks are committing more crimes and more serious crimes, this is hardly attributable to changing sex roles, since this societal group has not been restricted by sex role definitions in the past (Staples 1971). This research will determine whether there has been a change in the racial and social class distribution of offenders over time. It will also compare the seriousness of offenses of different offender types in periods before and after the advent of the women's movement.

Adler's interviews suggest increased aggressiveness on the part of certain female offenders. It is hard to know whether statements of aggressiveness in criminal activity are a result of professionalism (that is, years of experience "on the job") or a product of a change in sex role socialization. This distinction is crucial, since a change in behavior that resulted from professionalization would not reflect the impact of sociocultural factors. Therefore, it is important to correlate, in different historical periods, seriousness of first offense and age, since sex role theory would predict over time both increasing seriousness of offense of first offenders and commission of first offense at an earlier age.

In addition, sex role theory predicts that, because of changes in socialization practices, younger offenders now would commit more serious offenses than older offenders. This pattern is explicable in terms of sex roles—the older offenders' behavior dictated by the old sex roles; the younger offenders' by the new.

Finally, the use of companions in the commission of crime will be examined. Reckless (1957) was among the first to note that male delinquents were more likely to have companions than females. This, too, was interpreted as a result of sex roles.

> In the first place, the factor of companionship occurs much less frequently in female delinquency and crime than in male delinquency and crime. Women are not so likely to be involved in two-some, three-some, four-some crime; they are more likely to be lone-wolf doers. Here again this is the operation of culture pattern and role. [1957, p. 5]

These research questions then arise in examining peer networks: Are males more likely than females to engage in delinquency with friends? Are girls more likely now than in the past to be with companions when committing crimes? Are these companions more likely to be male or female? Does the sex composition of the group affect the seriousness of the crime committed?

In sum, sex role theory predicts that changing sex roles will affect the extent of female crime and the kind of individuals who commit crime. The new female criminal should be younger, of a higher social class, more likely to be white, capable of committing a more serious offense, and more inclined to be part of a group.

A control group of males has been used to recognize the effect of factors other than the women's movement's influence on sex roles and socialization practices. Presumably, other factors that influence crime rates, such as increased availability of drugs and the period effects of inflation and unemployment, have affected males as well as females, but changing sex roles have influenced only women's participation in criminal activity.

However, there is a competing alternative hypothesis to explain arrest-rate increases that is more difficult to eliminate. The activity of females may not have changed but the administration of justice may have. That is, the police may be more willing to arrest women than previously. Sex role images may have changed sufficiently to influence police perception of female culpability. The behavior of women may not have changed but the behavior of police toward women may have. Simon (1975) maintains that a distinct pattern of crime-arrest increases would deny the validity of this hypothesis. She argues that a change in police behavior would be reflected in a uniform increase in arrests for all offenses. This is not consistent with what is known of police practices and attitudes. Simon contends, "Why should the police be more willing to pick up women for larceny than murder?" (1975, p. 33). However, studies have shown that police variability is least evident where more serious violent and felony offenses are involved (Arnold 1971; Green 1970; McEachern and Bauzer 1967; Terry 1967; Thornberry 1973). The police, according to this research, have shown the greatest discretion with reference to the less serious property and Type II offenses.* This is where the greatest increases in arrests have been noted (Simon 1975, pp. 35-49). Therefore, this hypothesis cannot be disregarded, and intensive interviews with police officials are here used to determine the effect that changes in police procedures and personnel may have had on the offender population.

SIGNIFICANCE

This research is distinctive in that it studies female offenders by testing established theory that explores the dynamics of social change. Sociology has been criticized for being the study of male society. The field of criminology is especially sensitive to this criticism. The theoretical literature has focused almost exclusively on explaining male delinquency and crime. The continued choice of males as preferred subjects for empirical research has meant that most research generalizes only to the male population. This research attempts to modify this tradition. Even without the recent focus on the sex variable in the theoretical literature that has led to the development of new paradigms (Harris 1977), this would be a worthwhile undertaking if only to correct the discipline's male bias and bring the study of female delinquency up-to-date with the theoretical and empirical work on males. A simple psychological or "personal problems" approach to male delinquency gave way decades ago to a more sociological focus. Perhaps the study of female crime will progress similarly.

Too often, theory proliferates without adequate testing. While inductive theory may be grounded in empirical data (Glaser and Strauss 1966), it must still pass the test of independent verification (Blalock 1960). This research will probe the etiological theories that focus on the impact of the women's movement in changing sex-role-related attitudes and behaviors that influence female criminal activity. There is a clear need to test or probe a theory lest it be assumed

---

*The Federal Bureau of Investigation divides crimes into two categories. Type I offenses are the most serious by nature or by the volume in which they occur. They include criminal homicide, manslaughter, rape, robbery, aggravated assault, burglary, larceny, and auto theft. Type II offenses include other assaults, arson, forgery, counterfeiting, fraud, embezzlement, stolen property (buying, receiving, possessing), vandalism, weapons, prostitution, drug law violation, gambling, drunkenness, disorderly conduct, and vagrancy.

valid as it goes unchallenged. Through testing, a science maintains its credibility and keeps itself honest. Is the "new female criminal" a social invention or an empirical reality?

Most important, by collecting longitudinal data, the dynamics of social change are explored. Social science has tended toward what one methodologist called "temporal provincialism," since "85% of present day research refers to only one point in time" (Smith 1975, p. 276). By collecting longitudinal data, our understanding of the historical process is enlarged. A diachronic (across-time) analysis is essential to a more rigorous examination of the relationship between social movements and changes in delinquent behavior. Finally, the fact that no study with this intent or data base has ever been done on males or females makes this research an important attempt to expand our understanding of the etiology of crime.

2

METHODOLOGY

INTRODUCTION

The data base used for this study is a probability sample of arrests drawn from police records in a metropolitan city in New Jersey, known here as Metroville. For the years 1939, 1949, 1959, 1969, and 1976, data were collected on a systematic probability sample of 200 males and 200 females. In those years when the population of females arrested was less than 200, data were collected on the entire population. The entire criminal career of each person in the sample was traced through police and probation department records. The final sample includes 1,651 arrests: 519 female arrests and 1,132 male arrests.

Police arrest records and probation department files were searched for information on the following variables: age, sex, race, address, offense in the year of sampling, number and sex of companions involved in that offense (if any), role of respondent in the offense, and criminal record—including extent and type of previous and subsequent offenses. Initially, it was hoped that information could be gained on the education, family status, marital status, and employment history of each subject. However, this information was not systematically included in the arrest reports or probation department files.

CHOICE OF SITE

The choice of a research site hinged on two factors: the availability of arrest records for juveniles and adults over a 40-year period and the willingness of a chief of police to allow these records to be used for research purposes. Old records and records on juveniles are usually destroyed after a period of time. In addition, most police chiefs are not anxious to have their files reviewed by social scientists. Nevertheless, with the help of a county planning agency, the cooperation of the police and the probation department was forthcoming in Metroville.

It is important to note that Metroville is both economically and ethnically diverse. It had a median income in 1970 of $11,483, and 23 percent of its population then was black. At that time the median income for the county was $13,421 and for all Standard Metropolitan Statistical Areas (SMSAs), $9,943. Metroville is divided into census tracts that are quite different in their economic and occupational profiles; median income ranged in 1970 from $8,813 to $14,277 and percent unemployed, from 0.5 to 5.5.

Metroville is typical in that it is one of 1,385 other cities of similar size (U.S., Department of Commerce, Bureau of the Census 1977, p. 18). The extent of racial, ethnic, and social class differentiation found there is not unique. Cities like New York and Newark, New Jersey, are perhaps more intriguing criminoligically, but less typical of cities in the rest of the nation than suburban centers like Metroville.

CHOICE OF DATA: ARREST REPORTS

It is unfortunately true that in criminology any data base is defective. One chooses from a variety of imperfect data bases. Officially, there is the Federal Bureau of Investigation's Uniform Crime Reports (UCR) or, dropping down a level of bureaucracy, the police arrest records. The main source of unofficial data is the self-report studies of delinquency generated by social scientists. It is easy to debunk any data base; it is much harder to weigh relative disadvantages and settle on the better (though imperfect) source.

The Uniform Crime Reports are criticized for reflecting the confounding influences of variations in police enforcement practices and racial and class biases (Cressey 1957; Hartjen 1974; Piliavin and Briar 1964; Sellin 1951; Wolfgang 1963). Moreover, arrest statistics do not represent the universe of all those who commit crimes, but rather the nonrandomly distributed chance of being caught for criminal activity. When relying on police data, one recognizes that officially recorded misconduct is only the "visible illegal conduct" and that there is no way of estimating with confidence the extent of unreported, unrecorded, or undetected offenses. This "hidden crime" or the "dark figure of crime" has been extensively investigated (Biderman and Reiss 1967; Empey and Erickson 1966; Erickson and Empey

1963; Gibson 1967; Gold 1966; Short and Nye 1958; Vaz 1966). It is well recognized that most of us are part of that hidden crime statistic.

While delinquent conduct is far more widespread than official records suggest, studies indicate the direction of the bias. It is the most serious and frequent offender who is most likely to be arrested (Hood and Sparks 1970). Whereas most people do something at some time against the law, researchers in this area feel "a low proportion admit to persistent misbehavior" (1970, p. 51) that is undetected. If one compared respondents' reports of their own misbehavior (known as self-report studies) with self-estimates of future delinquent behavior with the number of past official court appearances, one finds a fairly high relationship between official and unofficial criteria of delinquency. Short and Nye (1970), in comparing unrecorded delinquency with official records of delinquency, find that the offenses for which boys most often admit involvement are the same offenses for which they are most often arrested. This suggests that arrest records are not totally invalid representations of criminal activity (Erickson 1972).

Whereas arrest records are criticized as representing only officially defined misconduct and, therefore, as more suitable for a study of the behavior of social control agents than a study of the offender population (Gove 1975; Hartjen 1974; Lemert 1967; Quinney 1970), self-report studies are also criticized for methodological defects. Problems of reliability, concealment, and exaggeration as well as sampling inaccuracies perturb these studies (Clark and Tifft 1966; Dentler 1963; Hardt and Bodine 1965). Moreover, court records exclude less serious offenders who are handled extrajudicially by the police and the probation department and reflect other discretionary aspects of the criminal justice system, such as plea bargaining. Samples of institutionalized populations are especially biased toward the lower-class, nonwhite, serious, and frequent offender. For this reason, etiological studies are severely criticized for using samples of incarcerated offenders to generalize to the larger population of offenders. To limit oneself to court-determined delinquency or incarcerated offenders introduces too many biases (Goldman 1963; Green 1970; Terry 1967; Thornberry 1973). Therefore, while recognizing the problems in available data, it seemed advisable to utilize the procedurally earliest source of recorded information about offenders —that is, police records.

Since this is a longitudinal study, the advantages of available data are crucial. The use of arrest records means there are no subject refusals that can distort the representativeness of the sample. Gaining continued cooperation and availability of subjects is unnecessary. There is no panel mortality, and the effect on response patterns and behavior of repeated interviewing is eliminated. By

using cross-sectional probability samples of arrests in different years
to define the sample and police and probation records to supply the
criminal record, the need for retrospective interview data is avoided.
Inaccuracies in remembering an offense history are eliminated. In
addition, facts such as age and address can be cross-checked easily.

Many scholars in the field (Glenn and Zody 1970; Hammond
1969; Orback 1961; Riley and Foner 1968) suggest cohort analysis to
avoid the weakness of the static cross-sectional study and the inaccuracies of retrospective accounts. Whereas retrospective accounts
based on interviews suffer from inaccuracies in subject recall and
nonprobability sampling bias, cross-sectional analyses present a static
view of behavior that can result in misinterpretation. Cross-sectional
analyses assume that differences in the activity patterns of younger
and older subjects are due to an aging process, ignoring the impact
of period and cohort effects. That is, cross-sectional studies are
not able to distinguish between aging effects (patterns due to life-cycle
change), cohort effects (generational effects or the differences in
aging due to the uniqueness of each cohort and the historical period
through which it passes), or period effects (effects that cut across
all age strata simultaneously). Riley and Foner note the difficulty of
disentangling life-cycle change from social change.

> The cross-section analysis, as we have seen, focuses upon
> different cohorts or persons who are of different ages at
> given points of time . . . and yields data essential for un-
> derstanding the age structure of the society. Since this
> form of analysis does not focus on life-cycle patterns,
> however, it provides no direct answers to questions about
> how the individual ages. . . . A good deal of research,
> failing to distinguish between cross-sectional and longi-
> tudinal views, attempts to reduce one to the other. As a
> consequence, there is considerable danger of fallacious
> interpretation, of erroneously inferring that differences
> among age categories in the society are due to the aging
> of individuals. [1968, p. 7]

In criminology, longitudinal studies of birth cohorts are rare.
Perhaps the most well known is Wolfgang, Figlio, and Sellin's (1972)
study of delinquency in a birth cohort. These researchers trace the
official delinquent career, up to age 18, of male juveniles born in
1945. Delinquents are compared with nondelinquents and the volume,
frequency, and character of delinquent careers are examined. This
longitudinal study concerns males only. There are no longitudinal
studies of females. More important, there are no studies of males
or females that compare delinquents from several birth cohorts as

this research attempts. The practical difficulties of such studies are undoubtedly the major reason for their infrequent use in delinquent research. Yet, Riley and Foner note the importance of such research.

> In order to understand the subtle interplay of individual aging and social change, it is necessary to use research methods that are more imaginative than those ordinarily employed. Thus, analyses tracing the life course, not of one, but of a sequence of cohorts, can broaden the understanding afforded by either of the two approaches (cross section study and the analysis of life cycle of single cohort) discussed. On the one hand, the description of the life pattern of a particular cohort cannot in itself reveal the inherent character of the life cycle process because with the passage of time, individuals are simultaneously affected by their own aging and by the trend of social and environmental events. . . . In order to isolate the effects of aging from the effects of social change, it is necessary to study the way in which different cohorts age at different times, in different places and under different conditions. . . . It is the flow of successive cohorts through the social structure that allows deeper understanding of social change, since the sequence of cohorts is a major channel for the transformation of society. [1968, pp. 9-10]

By using a series of cross-sectional probability samples of offenders, one is able to see the "flow of successive cohorts" that Riley describes.

The unavailability of comparable secondary data that cover a sufficient span of time is a frequent problem in cohort studies. Indeed, the use of arrest records may be problematic because of the unavailability of records for previous years or because of changes in police procedures that affect the likelihood of arrest. Changes in record keeping or police personnel or police arrest policies can reduce the comparability of data from previous years. Cognizant of these problems, intensive interviews with police personnel regarding changes in the police force were conducted. In the interpretation of data, information gained from these interviews will be explicitly stated.

CAPTURING THE COHORTS

First, it was necessary to define the size of the probability sample and to select the years from which the sample would be drawn.

TABLE 2.1

Number of Arrests Sampled by Year and Sex

Sex	1939	1949	1959	1969	1976	Total
Male	187	333	234	200	178	1,132
Female	25	24	63	210	197	519
Total	212	357	297	410	375	1,651

Source: Compiled by the author.

It was determined that a sample of 200 males and 200 females would be selected from the specified years. When the number of arrested females did not reach 200, the entire population was drawn. Table 2.1 indicates the size of the sample for each year.

As was indicated in Chapter 1, while the primary focus of this research is on changes in the frequency and character of female crime, a sample of males was drawn as a control group. This was done in the hope of understanding which period changes are sex-specific rather than being related to universal change agents.

There are several factors that influenced the choice of years from which the arrest records would be sampled: the need for complete data, the importance of capturing years both before and after the initial thrust of the women's movement, and the desire to reduce the impact of changes in police personnel that might have influenced the likelihood of arrest.

Data collection began in June 1977. Arrest records for 1976 were the first chosen to be sampled, since they represented the most current and complete file. For three reasons, the next year chosen was 1969: it represented an important year for the women's movement, the juvenile bureau was under the same leadership in 1969 as it was in 1976, and complete records of juvenile contacts were available in the personal logbook of the juvenile officer. A very brief history of both the women's movement and Metroville's police department might be helpful here.

Although interest in the rights of women has ebbed and flowed since the nineteenth-century suffrage movement, the nascence of the current movement, alternately termed women's lib, the women's liberation movement, the women's rights movement, or just the women's movement, is thought to be 1963. Historians of the movement (Freeman 1973) generally give the following events significance in leading to the development and popular impact of the movement.

In 1963 President Kennedy's Commission on the Status of Women issued its report (American Women) following two years of investigation under the leadership of Eleanor Roosevelt. This report, documenting the rights and opportunities denied women at that time, led to the establishment of 50 state commissions to do similar research on a state level. Freeman, while noting the probable political-patronage origins of these commissions, indicated their importance for the growth of the new women's movement.

> These commissions laid the groundwork for the future movement in three significant ways: (1) it brought together many knowledgeable, politically active women who otherwise would not have worked together around matters of direct concern to women; (2) the investigations unearthed ample evidence of women's unequal status, especially their legal and economic difficulties, in the process convincing many previously uninterested women that something should be done; (3) the reports created a climate of expectations that something would be done. . . . These commissions thus created an embryonic communications network among people with similar concerns. [1973, pp. 797-98]

In addition, Freeman notes two other events of significance: the publication in 1963 of Betty Friedan's The Feminine Mystique, and the addition of "sex" to Title VII of the 1964 Civil Rights Act (Freeman 1973, p. 798). The Feminine Mystique stimulated many women to question the status quo, and the hesitance of the Equal Employment Opportunity Commission (EEOC) to act on sex discrimination prompted some women within EEOC to lobby for "some sort of NAACP for women to put pressure on the government" (Freeman 1973, p. 798). As a result, on June 30, 1966, the National Organization for Women (NOW) was formed. Freeman describes the occasion.

> The occasion was the last day of the Third National Conference of Commissions on the Status of Women, ironically titled "Targets for Action." The opportunity came with a refusal by conference officials to bring to the floor a proposed resolution that urged the EEOC to give equal enforcement to the sex provision of Title VII as was given to the race provision. Despite the fact that these state commissions were not federal agencies, officials replied that one government agency could not be allowed to pressure another. The small group of women . . . had met the night before in Friedan's hotel room to discuss the possibility of a civil rights organization for women. Not

convinced of its need, they chose instead to propose the
resolution. When the resolution was vetoed, the women
held a whispered conversation over lunch and agreed to
form an action organization "to bring women into full
participation in the mainstream of American society
now, assuming all the privileges and responsibilities
thereof in truly equal partnership with men." The name
NOW was coined by Friedan, who was at the conference
researching her second book. Before the day was over,
28 women paid $5.00 each to join. [1973, p. 799]

In October 1967 the organizing conference was held with over
300 men and women charter members. Describing its original membership, Freeman notes that occupationally, the original members
were from the professions, labor, government, and the communications industry.

Instead of organizational experience, what the early NOW
members had was media experience, and it was here that
their early efforts were aimed . . . [NOW] was highly
successful in getting publicity, much less so in bringing
about concrete changes. [1973, p. 799]

Their efforts to stimulate membership culminated in a media blitz in
1969.

Historians have noted that the women's movement has always
had two branches: an older more conservative one, and a younger,
more radical, more informal network. The younger branch consisted
of women who had spent years in social-action projects and the 1960s
protest activities. These women "were quickly shunted into traditional roles and faced with the self-evident contradiction of working
in a 'freedom movement' without being free" (Freeman 1975, p. 57).
These women started organizing as early as 1964, but not until 1967
and 1968 did the "groups develop a determined, if cautious, continuity
and begin to consciously expand themselves" (1973, p. 800). Once
again, it was the realization that feminist concerns were not taken
seriously that led these women to break off from the larger leftist or-
ganizations of which they were a part to form their own network.
Groups emerged out of the anger generated by the 1967 National Conference for New Politics and the 1968 Seattle Students for a Demo-
cratic Society (SDS) meetings. These younger, radical, more public
groups were also featured in the 1969 media blitz.

In this brief history of the new women's movement, we see that
although organizing efforts began as early as 1964, the media did not
transmit the message of the movement with much vigor until 1969.

By then, however, the movement was fully recognized, and by 1970 there was much publicity of the alleged impact of its ideology in such widely read publications as Transaction, Newsweek, the New York Times, Time, and Psychology Today. Thus, 1969 seemed an appropriate year to sample in terms of sex role theory.

It was also a good year from the point of view of organizational pressures in Metroville's police department. Metroville's police force has grown over the years as the population it covers has expanded. Its expansion has been similar to that of other police forces across the country. The most significant change in the department occurred in its handling of juvenile offenders. In 1953 the department started keeping separate records for juveniles. Previously, they were handled informally. That is, a reproval or warning might have been given, but rarely was an arrest report filed. Because of this practice, a very small number of juveniles are included in the arrests for the years 1939 and 1949. From 1953 to 1977 there have been three juvenile officers: the first served from 1953 through 1961; the second, from 1962 until 1968; and the third, from 1968 until January 1977.

Assuming that organizational changes in the police department and concomitant changes in the likelihood of arrest are an uncontrolled variable affecting arrest statistics, the confounding influence of this factor was eliminated when possible. Since 1969 was a significant year for the women's movement and also a year in which the 1976 juvenile officer had been in charge, this year was selected as the second year to be sampled. While it may certainly be true that an officer's attitudes and behavior change during the course of the years, there is probably less difference over time in one officer's approach to law enforcement than there is between the attitudes and behavior of two different officers.

In addition, census statistics, which are used in the analysis and coding of socioeconomic status, are based on data collected in the ninth year of the decade. For this reason it was optimal to use arrest statistics compiled in those years. Also, the interpretation of cohort analysis customarily dictates the selection of ten-year intervals between samples. In accordance with this practice and moving backwards in time, then, 1959, 1949, and 1939 were selected as the years in which arrests would be sampled.

UNEARTHING THE DATA

Once the years to be sampled were determined, the search for the arrest files began. Original 1976 arrest reports were readily available for adults. The 1976 and 1969 juvenile data were drawn from the personal, chronological logbook of the juvenile officer. The original adult arrest reports for the specific years previous to 1974 could not be located, although the attic, basement, and storerooms of the Municipal Building were searched with the help of several officers. However, an alphabetical index of all offenders and all arrests since 1920 was still in existence, about to be dismantled and replaced by the computerized Lier system that is being adopted by many police departments across the country. This index was used to compile the arrest and previous record data of the samples for 1969, 1959, 1949, and 1939. Juvenile arrest records for the years 1957-67 were unearthed in a basement closet. These records have been used to show patterns in juvenile arrests between the sampled years of 1959 and 1969. The few juvenile records that were compiled in 1949 and 1939 were found mixed in with the adult records.

Once the initial sample of arrests was collected, the work of tracking the criminal career of each individual was begun. Information on an individual could be located in either police or probation department records. Within the police department, the following sources were reviewed: rap sheets, which provided an arrest history; the Lier files, which held a complete criminal history of anyone arrested in 1977; and the alphabetical offender file already mentioned. Within the county probation department, five overlapping file systems were located and reviewed for information on the juvenile careers of all offenders.

Note that since this research sampled arrests, not offenders, an individual might be included two or more times in a year's sample, depending on the extent and timing of the criminal activity. In this study there are 1,651 sample arrests and 1,455 individual offenders. Arrests, not offenders, were sampled in order to make this study compatible with other secondary analyses of Uniform Crime Reports statistics, all of which have taken this approach. Moreover, in some years arrest files were organized in chronological order. It would have been impossible, therefore, to collect a probability sample of offenders without rearranging the police department's files. This seemed inadvisable.

THE AVAILABILITY OF INFORMATION

Adult and juvenile records are kept separately and contain different information. The official adult arrest report has space to include information on the following variables: name, age, birth date, race, sex, address, offense charged, time of arrest, date of arrest, details of offense and arrest, bail, disposition, offender's employer, an arrest number, a complaint number, the statutory code number of offense, name of officer making the arrest, name of the complainant, and employer of the complainant. However, this information is not always complete. Juvenile arrests are recorded on arrest cards that include information on age, sex, race, name of offender, offense charged, and details of the offense.

Generally speaking, reliable and valid information was obtainable on name, age, birth date, address, race, sex, and offense for adults. For juveniles, name, race, age, sex, address, birth date, offense, and number and sex of companions were available. In the following sections, the extent of information on companions, the measure of social class, and the coding of seriousness of offense are discussed.

Extent of Companionship

It was not possible to ascertain the extent of peer companionship in adult offenses. However, this research is more concerned with the sex and number of companions in juvenile offenses, since it is among adolescents that peer-group networks typically influence offense seriousness and frequency (Cohen 1955; Hood and Sparks 1970). The social context in which delinquent acts occur has been previously researched, primarily in terms of gang involvement. No data on gang involvement was collected; gang activity in Metroville is practically nonexistent. However, the number and sex of companions participating in each juvenile offense in 1959, 1969, and 1976 were of interest and were collected. This information was directly available for 1959 from the arrest cards on which details of the offense were given. For 1969 and 1976 juvenile offenses, the number and sex of companions could be deduced from the complaint numbers, since all juveniles involved in the same offense received the same complaint number. It is possible, of course, that juveniles were present and involved but fled and were not arrested. Whereas this undoubtedly happened sometimes, it is assumed such was not the case frequently, and the errors here are due to chance rather than systematic favoritism.

Measuring Socioeconomic Status

One objective of this study is to investigate any change in the relationship between social class and offense frequency and seriousness. The information on arrest records did not consistently include data on family income, occupation of family head, or employment status of the offender—the more conventional indexes of socioeconomic status. However, address was always available, and with the aid of enlarged census maps and street directories, it was possible to locate

TABLE 2.2

Rossi's Seriousness Scores for Offenses

Score	Offense
3.53	Traffic, drunk and disorderly, disorderly, possessing a dangerous weapon, truancy, incorrigibility, runaway, lottery, vagrancy, possessing alcoholic beverages, offensive language, attempted suicide, desertion, abandonment
5.14	Malicious damage, possessing stolen property, shoplifting, insufficient funds, larceny under $200
5.45	Violation of probation, obscene phone calls, contributing to the delinquency of a minor, fugitive
5.62	Glue sniffing, possession of drugs, prostitution
5.67	Fraud and forgery, larceny undefined
6.21	Auto theft, larceny over $200, burglary
6.39	Arson
6.57	Assault
6.97	Assault on a police officer
7.12	Causing death by auto
7.18	Attrocious assault, carnal abuse, rape, incest
7.27	Drugs: intent to sell
7.33	Robbery, armed robbery
7.37	Manslaughter, murder

Source: Rossi, Waite, Bose, and Berk, "The Seriousness of Crimes: Normative Structure and Individual Differences," American Sociological Review 39 (April 1974): 232.

any address in an appropriate census tract. The 120 census tracts were then rank ordered based on the census variable "median income of families and unrelated individuals."

Once a measure of social class is derived, it is then necessary to specify cutting points to designate different social classes. Almost any cutting points that may be used are to some degree arbitrary. The dividing points finally employed emerged after alternate approaches were explored. In the end, Wolfgang, Figlio, and Sellin's (1972) approach of settling on two socioeconomic categories, designated "higher" and "lower," divided by the median income for families and unrelated individuals of the most appropriate geographic unit (in their case, Philadelphia; in this case, the county) was used. Wolfgang, Figlio, and Sellin collapse the five social class categories into lower and higher socioeconomic status "to simplify the treatment, because the more refined distinctions among the five categories were minimal and cell size in the upper categories was often small" (1972, p. 53). For these reasons and because further distinctions between social classes would have been quite arbitrary, only two social classes were designated for each year.

	Social Class	
Date	Lower	Higher
1976 and 1969	0-$9,943	$9,944-
1959	0-$6,267	$6,268-

Social class distinctions were not calculated for the 1939 or 1949 data, since there were no census tracts then, and therefore, all the town residents would fall into one social class. This did not appear to be a fine enough scale to merit consideration.

Determining a Measure of Seriousness of Offense

While the details of an arrest are not always available, the offense and its statutory code always are. For much of the analysis, this nominal measure or an ordinal measure developed by grouping victimless, property, and personal offenses was used. An interval measure of seriousness of offense was required, however, for the cohort analysis.

Building on the pioneering work of Sellin and Wolfgang (1964),* Rossi, Waite, Bose, and Berk (1974) developed a measure of the se-

----

*Sellin and Wolfgang (1964) have developed a measure of delinquency that has received wide recognition and replication (Akman, Normandeau, and Turner 1967; Figlio 1975; Normandeau 1966; Wellford and Wiatrowski 1975). This index evaluates the comparative seriousness of a delinquent event by taking into account its various components and assigning weights to each event that produced injury to a victim and/or some loss of or damage to property. The total event is then given a single numerical score value. This technique is unique; the Uniform Crime Reports classification of offenses does not include the possible components of an event, rather, only the most serious component of a complex event. In addition, legal labels are so broad that they may cover a spectrum of events that differ in actual degree of harm inflicted on the individual or community.

riousness of criminal acts by examining the nature and degree of popular consensus concerning a sample of 140 criminal acts. In their own words, they try to get at "what it is about criminal acts which leads them to be regarded as more or less serious in the popular eye" (1974, p. 225). They find that "collectively respondents are reacting to the simple characteristics of the crimes they rated" (1974, p. 233; emphasis added). That is, the extent of damage inflicted is not as important as the type of damage, whether it be to people rather than property, for example. Because of the extent of subgroup consensus, Rossi, Waite, Bose, and Berk developed a crime classification system based on the variation from crime to crime in the average ratings given to the 140 crimes in their representative sample of 200 Baltimore residents. This crime classification system orders crimes by seriousness, and it is used here as an interval measure of seriousness. Table 2.2 indicates scale scores for each offense based on unstandardized regression coefficients for 11 binary variables (1974, p. 232).

If details of all offenses in all the years were available, it would have been possible to use the Sellin-Wolfgang index. However, police reports do not usually provide the extensive information that this scale requires—that is, the dollar amount of damage inflicted or property taken, the nature of force used whether it be verbal or physical, and the extent of physical harm incurred (was the victim hospitalized or was he/she treated and discharged). Even if these details could have been unearthed for current (1976) offenses by examining original complaints, the information would not have been available for offenses committed in previous years. Consequently, a simpler scale had to be utilized.

3

AN EXAMINATION OF
CHANGES IN THE
QUANTITY OF FEMALE CRIME

INTRODUCTION

The first question to be answered is, Has there been a real increase in female crime over time? Naturally, any increase is relative and must be interpreted in light of changes in comparative groups. Researchers have addressed this question by using Uniform Crime Reports (UCR) data to examine nationwide changes in the arrest rate and the proportion of women arrested (the sex ratio).

Giordano notes that between 1960 and 1973 the national arrest rate for females under 18 increased 264 percent for all offenses, 393 percent for violent offenses, and 334 percent for property offenses, compared with male increases of 124 percent, 236 percent, and 82 percent, respectively (Giordano 1976, pp. 14-18). Increases for specific offenses are noted by Adler (1975). She stresses that between 1960 and 1972

> the number of women arrested for robbery rose 277 percent, while the male figure rose 169 percent. Dramatic differences are found in embezzlement (up to 280 percent for women, 50 percent for men), larceny (up 303 percent for women, 82 percent for men), and burglary (up 168 percent for women, 63 percent for men). [1975, p. 16]

ANALYTIC APPROACH

Trends in Metroville were examined to determine if increases in the extent of crime there parallel the increases nationwide. Paramount were (1) examining the percentage increase from 1939 to 1976 in the number of females arrested, using males as a control group; (2) determining the extent to which any trends were accelerating or decelerating; (3) computing the proportion of the crime-prone-age-group population that was arrested, as a function of time; and (4) determining the extent to which any increase over time in number of arrests also meant an increase in the number of offenders (or individuals) arrested.

Nationwide, the Federal Bureau of Investigation (FBI) data attest to changes in the arrest rate, as previously cited. However, researchers thus far have placed less emphasis on the extent to which a trend is accelerating or decelerating (as in 2 above) and on examining arrest rates in the light of demographic changes (3 above).

In addition, increases in arrests are implicitly assumed to imply corresponding increases in the number of individuals arrested (see 4 above), without proper justification. Frequently researchers use the terms arrests and offenders interchangeably. For example, Adler uses UCR statistics to conclude that "the number of women arrested for robbery rose by 277 percent" (1975, p. 16; emphasis added). But the Uniform Crime Reports contain data only on the number of arrests, not the number of individuals arrested. * Changes in the number of arrests do not necessarily correlate strongly with changes in the number of women involved in criminal activity. For example, a marked increase in frequency of arrests within a constant (in number) criminal population would also explain rising arrest rates. The extent to which this is true in these data will be determined.

RESEARCH RESULTS

It is important to recognize that if sex role changes are primarily responsible for increased female criminal activity, long-term trends should be expected to follow the pattern illustrated in Figure 3.1. That is, a fairly stable pattern is interrupted by a sharp increase in arrests as sex role changes affect criminal activity. However, the data for Metroville indicate that increases in arrests actually began in the 1949-59 period. It appears that this decade, which was marked by a postwar return to traditional sex roles (Freeman 1975), also was a time marked by increased female criminal activity.

Examination of the data on Metroville shows that it reflects in the 1959-69 period the nationwide picture that made media headlines.

---

*See U.S., Department of Justice, Federal Bureau of Investigation, U.S. Reporting Handbook: How to Prepare Uniform Crime Reports (Washington, D.C.: Government Printing Office, 1949, 1955, 1962, 1964, 1966, and 1971).

FIGURE 3.1

Hypothetical Arrest-Rate Index for Females
(1939 = 100)

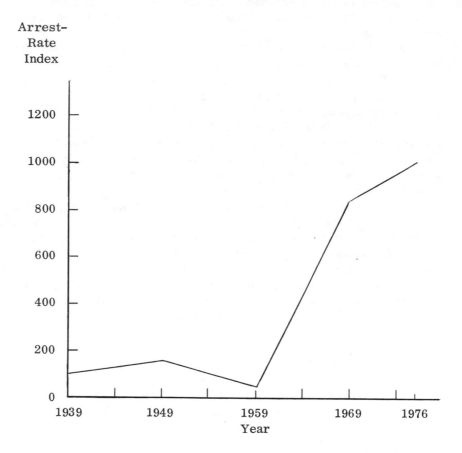

The headlines decreed the darker side of women's liberation to be an
increase in female crime. This alleged movement of females toward
parity with males in terms of incidence of crime, along with the shift
of women into more serious offense patterns, has been interpreted as
a consequence of changes in sex roles and social roles. According
to this argument, developments in the direction of sexual equality
have expanded crime opportunities and pressures toward criminal activity among women. However, the data on Metroville show that the
female crime patterns that have been cited as a consequence of the
women's movement actually began in the earlier decade 1949-59, a
period of quite traditional sex roles. That is, the trends that in
1959-69 are attributed to changing sex roles are also apparent in
1949-59.

Changes in Percentage Increase in Arrests
and Percentage Rate of Change

In Table 3.1 note that the numbers of arrests for women and men increased monotonically from 1939 to 1976.* In 1939 there were 25 female arrests compared with 303 in 1976. Male arrests jumped from 327 in 1939 to 1,424 in 1976.

Studies using national statistics have tended to focus on trends in the period 1959-69. Metroville mirrors the nation's image by showing greater percentage increases for women than for men in this period. Female arrests increased 367 percent from 1959 to 1969, compared with a male increase of 156 percent.

The increase is especially pronounced for white females (505 percent), compared with black females (169 percent). Moreover, comparing females with males within each racial group, there is a greater disparity between white females and males (505 percent versus 135 percent increases, respectively) than between black females and males (169 percent versus 218 percent increases, respectively). In addition, note that among women it is the juveniles, not the adults, who experience the greatest increase in arrests for this period. From 1959 to 1969, arrests of juvenile females jump 788 percent, compared with an increase of 75 percent for adult females and an increase of 426 percent for male juveniles.

Examining the arrest data (and changes therein) from 1939 to 1976 is especially interesting. While the increases in number of female arrests, and especially of juvenile female arrests, are marked in the decade 1959-69, a significant precursor occurs in the 1949-59 period.

In Figure 3.2 the total male and female arrest-rate index is compared. That is, total population arrest statistics are transformed into arbitrary units, with the 1939 arrest figures equal to 100. Interestingly, although the 1959-69 period shows a marked increase in arrests, this trend actually began between 1949 and 1959 and in the post-1969 period levels off. It is in the 1969-76 period where the "new female trend" would be expected to strengthen rather than level off if the women's movement were the driving force.

In Figure 3.3 these data are plotted to compare the average rate of percentage increase per annum in different periods. Clearly the increase in total female arrests is almost as great in the 1949-59 period (10.13 percent) as it is from 1959 to 1969 (16.5 percent). Note

---

*In this chapter, sample statistics have been extrapolated to represent population parameters. All calculations are based on figures for the entire population of offenders arrested in this town.

TABLE 3.1

Total Arrests and the Average Percentage Rate of Change per Annum for Selected Groups, 1939-76

	Number of Total Arrests					Average Percentage Rate of Change per Annum*			
	1939	1949	1959	1969	1976	1939-49	1949-59	1959-69	1969-76
Total									
Male	327	333	468	1,200	1,424	0.18	3.46	9.87	2.48
Female	25	24	63	294	303	-0.41	10.13	16.65	0.43
Adult									
Male	320	324	332	516	680	0.12	0.24	4.51	4.02
Female	24	20	36	63	126	-1.81	6.05	5.76	10.41
Juvenile									
Male	4	7	130	684	744	7.15	33.93	18.06	1.21
Female	1	1	26	231	177	0.00	38.52	24.41	-3.73
Black									
Male	84	93	136	432	784	1.02	3.87	12.25	8.89
Female	14	14	26	70	160	0.00	6.39	10.41	12.54
White									
Male	243	239	326	768	640	-0.17	3.15	8.95	-2.57
Female	11	9	37	224	137	-1.99	15.18	19.73	-6.78

*The average percentage rate of change per annum is, in effect, the "inflation rate" for crime. Technically, if 100P is defined as percentage rate of change divided by number of years and 100R is defined as average annual percentage rate of change, then $R = (NP + 1)^{1/N} - 1$.

Source: Compiled by the author.

FIGURE 3.2

Arrest-Rate Index for Males and Females
(1939 = 100)

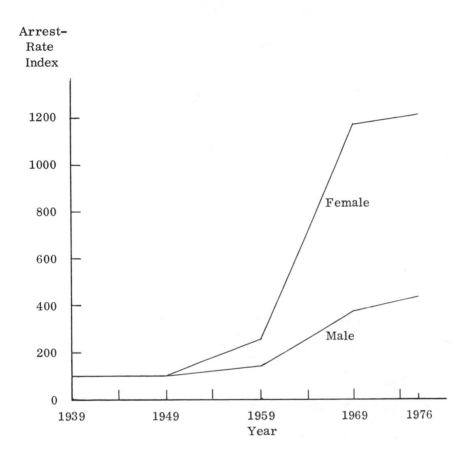

that from 1969 to 1976 there is a deceleration of the former trend. In that seven-year period, while the women's movement continues to effect sex role changes, the rate of average percentage increase in female arrests declines markedly.

Figure 3.4 allows a comparison of adult males and adult females. While the adult male arrest rate starts to rise in 1959, the adult female arrest rate started its climb and has been climbing more sharply than rates for males since that time. In fact, the difference between the 1969 and 1976 arrest rate is most dramatic.

A comparison of Figures 3.5 and 3.6 indicates that the activity of black males and females (Figure 3.5) over time has been more similar than the activity of white males and females (Figure 3.6).

FIGURE 3.3

A Comparison of Male and Female Crime Rates, Expressed in
Average Rate of Percentage Increase per Annum

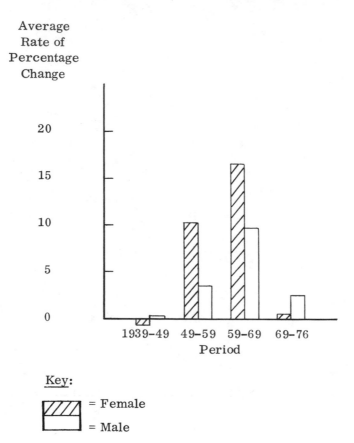

Key:

= Female
= Male

The arrest-rate index of white females increased most sharply from
1959 to 1969. But this trend is anticipated by an upswing in arrests
from 1949 to 1959. Black males and black females (Figure 3.5) have
responded in a similar pattern to etiological factors. The time of
greatest increase for blacks is the most recent 1969-76 period.

The comparison of white and black females in Figure 3.7 re-
veals that white females have a greater change in arrest activity than
blacks in both decades 1949-59 and 1959-69. Yet from 1969 to 1976,
the trend in black female arrests continues to rise, whereas the
trend in white female arrests drops off sharply.

Figure 3.8 indicates that the increase in female activity is
largely due to the activity of juvenile females. Compared with ju-

veniles, the arrest index for adult females has barely changed. More-over, a trend that began in the 1949-59 period is sharply accelerated between 1959 and 1969. A deceleration is shown in the arrest index of the juveniles in the period 1969-76.

Figure 3. 9 indicates that the relationship between juvenile and adult female arrests is similar to the relationship between juvenile and adult males. Among males, also, the greatest increases are among juveniles. However, for male juveniles only, the upward trend continues, though at a lesser pace, in the 1969-76 period.

Because the pattern for male and female juveniles is so similar from 1949 to 1969, an examination of yearly shifts is advisable. In Figure 3. 10, note the erratic pattern of juvenile arrests from 1957 to

FIGURE 3. 4

Arrest-Rate Index for Adult Males and Adult Females
(1939 = 100)

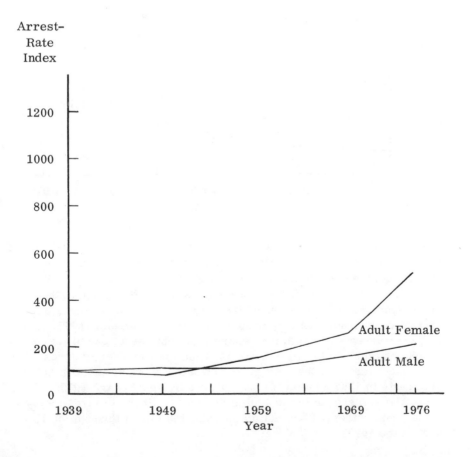

FIGURE 3.5

Arrest–Rate Index for Black Males and Black Females
(1939 = 100)

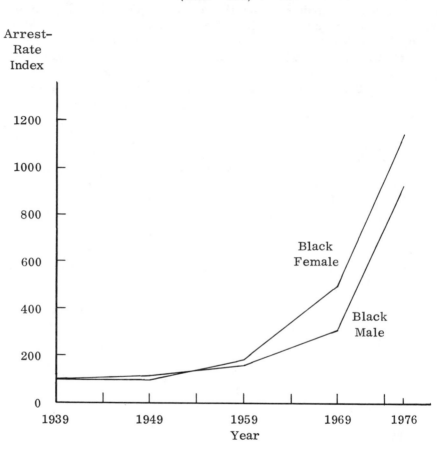

1967. A juvenile officer was first appointed in 1953. Records of
total juvenile arrests from 1957 to 1967 were available. A breakdown
of arrests by sex could be determined for the years 1959–67. While
many more males than females were arrested in this period, there
is no clear upward or downward trend for either sex. Rather, an
erratic up-and-down pattern prevails for both sexes until 1967. In
that year arrests began to rise sharply for both sexes, until they
reached a high of 915 in 1969. In 1976 the total number of arrests,
921, is not far from the 1969 mark. Whatever precipitated the rise
in arrests in 1967 continues through the early part of the 1970s. However, the arrest rate for juveniles has not continued to rise steeply
since 1969; rather, it has maintained the 1969 level through the first
part of the 1970s.

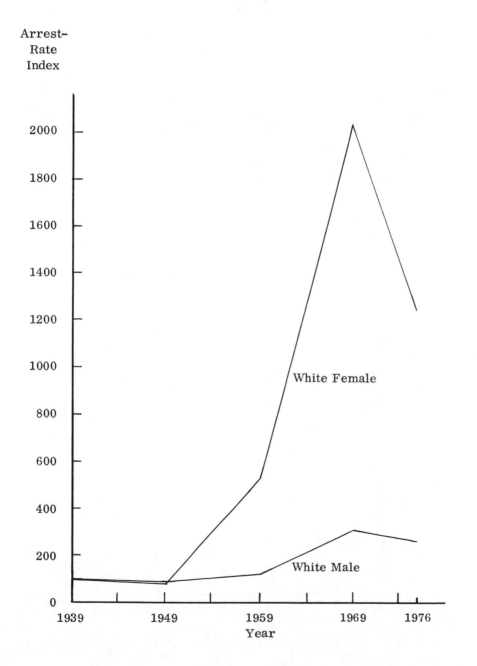

FIGURE 3.6

Arrest–Rate Index for White Males and White Females
(1939 = 100)

Arrest–
Rate
Index

White Female

White Male

Year

43

FIGURE 3.7

Arrest-Rate Index for White Females and Black Females
(1939 = 100)

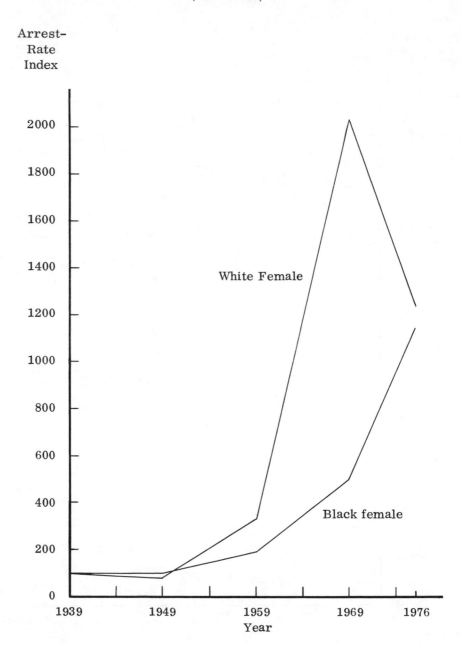

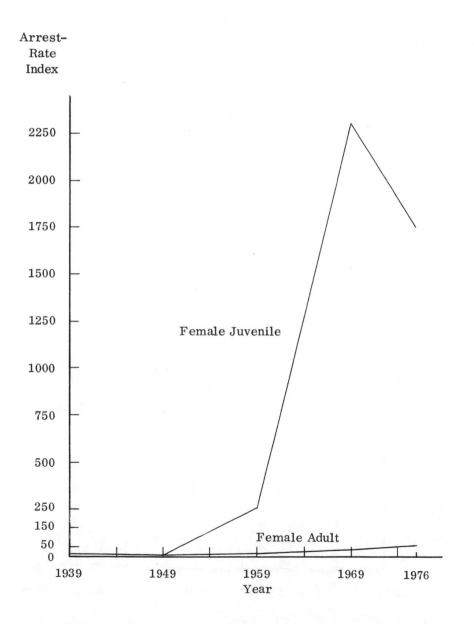

FIGURE 3.8

Arrest-Rate Index for Female Juveniles and Female Adults
(1939 = 10)

FIGURE 3.9

Arrest-Rate Index for Male Juveniles and Male Adults
(1939 = 10)

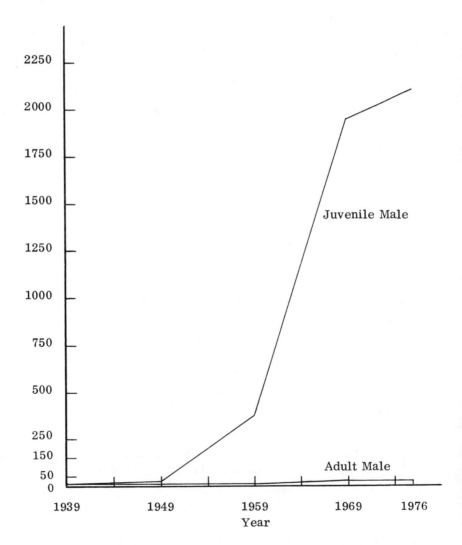

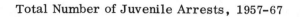

FIGURE 3.10

Total Number of Juvenile Arrests, 1957–67

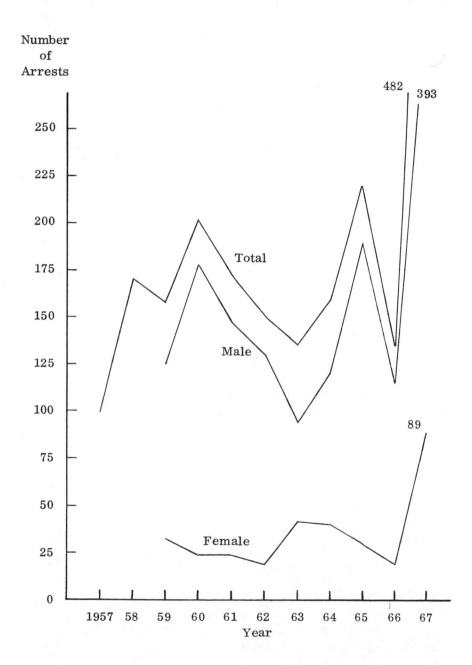

To what can we attribute this increase in juvenile arrests? Several interpretations are possible. Such an increase could have been precipitated by social changes or police procedural and administrative changes. With respect to social changes, it is hard to credit the women's movement with the change in the arrest index, since one would expect the message of the movement to affect girls' behaviors only. The fact that both sexes are affected similarly suggests some other social or administrative event is operative. To explore the possibility of changes in the administration of justice, informal interviews were conducted with police administrators and detectives. Since a change to a more zealous juvenile officer was effected in 1968, the possibility that law enforcement practices influenced the arrest rate can not be ruled out. The significance of the "change in police procedure" hypothesis will be examined as more of the data are discussed.

Sex Ratios

In examining national trends, much attention is given to the sex ratio. * The correlation between changes in the sex ratio and changes in the status of women is noted by Sutherland and Cressey.

> The sex ratio in crime tends to be lowest in countries
> in which females have the greatest freedom and equality
> with males, such as Western Europe, Australia, Canada
> and the United States, and to be the highest in countries
> in which females are closely supervised, such as Al-
> giers. . . . The extent to which the rate for males ex-
> ceeds the rate for females varies with the social posi-
> tions of the sexes in different groups within a nation.
> [1978, p. 132]

Nationwide the decline in the sex ratio is noted in several studies. Datesman, Scarpitti, and Stephenson cite the UCR 1971 ratio of male to female offenders as approximately 6:1; for juveniles, the sex ratio was 4:1 (1975, p. 107). Simon notes that the sex ratio for property offenses in 1953 was 12:1. In 1972 it dropped to 4.7:1. Specifically, burglary and auto theft were "male dominated offenses in 1972 as they were in 1953" (1975, p. 41). However, arrests for larceny, embezzlement, and fraud have shown striking changes.

---

*Sutherland and Cressey note that the declining sex ratio is supported generally by self-report studies (1978, p. 131). See also Hindelang (1971) and Weis (1976).

TABLE 3.2

Percentage of Females among Arrests, 1939-76

Year	Percentage of Females among Arrests
1939	7
1949	7
1959	12
1969	20
1976	19

Source: Compiled by the author.

In 1953, about 1 in every 20 arrests of women was for larceny. In 1972, the ratio was up to 1 in 5. For males, the proportion shifted from 1 in 27 to 1 in 12.2. . . . In 1972 approximately 1 in 4 persons arrested for forgery was a woman and 1 in 3.5 arrests for embezzlement and fraud involved a woman. [1975, p. 41]

In Metroville the sex ratio changed from 13:3 in 1939, to 7:1 in 1959, to 4:1 in 1969. The proportion of women who were arrested for all types of crime during the 1939-76 period is shown in Table 3.2. The percentage of females among arrests increased from a low of 7 percent in 1939 to a high of 20 percent in 1969. In other words, one of 14.3 arrests was a female in 1939 and 1949. Whereas, one of five arrests was a female in both 1969 and 1976. Computing an average rate of change, the period of greatest change is found to be 1959-69 (+.80 percent per year). The second period experiencing large change is 1949-59 (+.50 percent per year). From 1969 to 1976, there is negative change (-.14 percent per year). Interestingly, there is a greater average rate of change from 1949 to 1959 (+.50 percent) than there is from 1959 to 1976 (+.41 percent per year). Therefore, the periods 1949-59 and 1959-69 are the periods of greatest change.

Changes Examined in Light of Demographic Controls

Examining arrests per thousand population (Table 3.3), it becomes apparent that the trends noted in previous tables and graphs are not erased by controls for changes in population size.

Total arrests per thousand have been increasing since 1939; the average percentage rate of change per annum was greater (10.93) from

TABLE 3.3

Arrest Rate per Thousand Population and Its Average Percentage Rate of Change per Annum for Selected Groups, 1939-76

	Arrest Rate per Thousand					Average Percentage Rate of Change per Annum			
	1939	1949	1959	1969	1976	1939-49	1949-59	1959-69	1969-76
Total arrests	23.0	20.9	30.0	84.6	98.5	-1.0	3.7	10.9	2.2
Total									
Male	45.4	41.4	56.7	147.3	176.0	-0.9	3.2	10.0	2.6
Female	3.1	2.6	6.7	30.9	32.1	-1.6	9.7	16.6	0.5
Total									
White	18.4	16.1	23.9	73.3	57.9	-1.3	4.0	11.9	-3.3
Black	68.2	61.9	63.7	125.7	238.1	-0.97	0.3	7.0	9.6
Juvenile									
Male	1.8	3.1	50.6	278.0	304.7	5.6	32.1	18.6	1.3
Female	0.6	0.5	9.9	97.0	74.9	-2.5	36.0	25.6	-3.6
Adult									
Male	44.4	55.8	58.4	90.7	120.4	2.3	0.5	4.5	4.1
Female	3.0	2.9	5.3	8.8	17.8	-0.3	6.2	5.3	10.5

Source: Compiled by the author.

1959 to 1969. For men and women as a group and for whites, the period 1959-69 was the time of greatest change; the period from 1949 to 1959, the time of second greatest change. For juveniles, 1949-59 was the decade of greatest change, while 1959-69 was the second highest in percentage rate of change. In the most recent period, 1969-76, the adult female arrest rate experienced its greatest increase. For adult males, the period of greatest change was 1959-69. Among men, the juvenile arrest rate first exceeded the adult rate in 1969. However, among females, juveniles exceeded adults starting in 1959.

While the arrest rate per thousand has in each period been higher for males than females, the average percentage rate of change per annum is higher for females from 1949 to 1969. Finally, the white arrest rate from 1949 to 1969 shows an average rate of increase per year greater than that of blacks, although the arrest rate per thousand is higher for blacks than for whites through the period studied. * Essentially, then, the pattern of male-female arrests seen earlier is not changed when controls for changes in population size are introduced.

Arrests versus Offenders

In comparing the number of arrests with the number of offenders, the main concern here is in calling attention to the fact that the two are not synonymous. Because of FBI reporting procedures, police record numbers of arrests. As arrests increase, it is necessary to come to a better understanding of the role of the multiple offender.

Among juvenile females, the percentage of single offenders has been decreasing since 1959; consequently, the number of multiple offenders has been rising. The percentage of single offenders among all juvenile offenders has gone from 91 percent in 1959 to 87 percent in 1969 to 78 percent in 1976.

The pattern for female adults is not as clear. In 1939 and 1949, 96 percent of all offenders are single offenders. In 1959 that percentage drops to 79 percent, and in 1969 there is an increase to 93 percent single offenders. By 1976, 86 percent of female offenders

---

*Unfortunately a population breakdown of race by sex was not available in the 1970 census tracts. Communications with the County Planning Board and the Town Planning Board did not produce the missing data. Therefore, computations of arrest rate of black males, black females, white males, and white females for 1970 or 1976 were not possible.

are arrested just once in that year. If a greater percentage of single offenders in a given year is an indicant of more widespread criminality, then 1969 is a more serious year for female adults than is 1959 or 1976.

Unfortunately, there are not sufficient data on males to conduct a similar analysis.

CONCLUSION

In conclusion, an analysis of trends in the number of arrests from 1959 to 1976 indicates that while 1959-69 shows a marked increase in female arrests, 1949-59 is the precursor to this. For both sexes the greatest arrest increases are among juveniles, not adults. Whites show greater changes than blacks. However, the period 1969-76 shows a shift in these trends. Arrests among male and female adults rise, while juvenile activity slows down.

How may these empirical facts be interpreted? What theory (or theories) are consistent with the data? Sex role theory suggests (1) that changes in white female activity should be greater than changes in black female activity, (2) that juveniles will exhibit more change than adults, and (3) that female arrest patterns will change more than male arrest patterns.

While all these expectations are supported by the data, it is also true that the disparity between adult and juvenile arrests among females is also true among males. Furthermore, it is also the case that between 1949 and 1959 the female arrest rate rose faster than the male, that changes in criminal activity are greater among juveniles than among adults, and that white females experience higher arrest-rate increases than black females. Thus, all the trends that in 1959-69 are used in support of sex role theory are also true in 1949-59, a period when there was little sex role change and no women's movement.

4

AN EXAMINATION OF
CHANGES IN THE
TYPE OF OFFENDER AND
SERIOUSNESS OF OFFENSE

INTRODUCTION

From the demographic data presented in Chapter 3, it is evident
that there has been a real increase in the number of women committing crimes since 1939 that is not offset by demographic controls.
However, is there a "new female criminal?" That is, has the race,
social class, or type (in terms of criminal record) of offender
changed as the sex role theorists predict? Are more serious crimes
being committed now? Are offenders in 1969 and 1976 similar and
distinct from their counterparts in 1939, 1949, and 1959?

TRENDS IN THE SOCIAL CHARACTERISTICS
OF OFFENDERS

Racial Distribution

Table 4.1 shows that among males the percentage of arrests of
black offenders has been steadily increasing. The biggest increase
was from 1969 to 1976. Among females, however, the pattern is different. The percentage of blacks among offenders has not been
steadily increasing (see Table 4.2). There was a greater percentage
of arrests of black than white offenders in 1939 and 1949. In fact,
the percentage of black arrests rose slightly in that period. However,
in both 1959 and 1969 there was a greater percentage of arrests of
white female offenders than black. In 1969, especially, arrests of
white offenders represented three-quarters of the sample. It is interesting to note that this pattern, which began in 1959, is sharpened
in 1969 but is reversed in 1976. That is, among females in 1976, as

TABLE 4.1

Percentage Distribution of Male Arrests by Race and Year

| Race | Year | | | | |
	1939	1949	1959	1969	1976
Black	25.7	28.0	29.4	36.0	55.1
White	74.3	72.0	70.6	64.0	44.9
Total percent	100	100	100	100	100
Total number	187	332	231	200	178

Note: $x^2 = 48.96024$, $p = .0000$.

Source: Compiled by the author.

TABLE 4.2

Percentage Distribution of Female Arrests by Race and Year

| Race | Year | | | | |
	1939	1949	1959	1969	1976
Black	56.0	60.9	41.3	23.8	53.9
White	44.0	39.1	58.7	76.2	46.1
Total percent	100	100	100	100	100
Total number	25	23	63	210	193

Note: $x^2 = 45.10730$, $p = .000$.

Source: Compiled by the author.

in 1939 and 1949, blacks are responsible for a larger percentage of the population of arrests.

Social Class Distribution

In Table 4.3 the social class distribution of males and females for the years 1959, 1969, and 1976 are compared. In all three years, for males and females, a greater percentage of offenders were from the lower rather than the higher social class. However, as the sex role theorists would predict, the percentage of female offenders from the higher social classes was much greater in 1969 (41.7 percent) than in 1959 (29.8 percent). Yet, in 1976 there is a drop in the number of higher-social-class female offenders. The social class distribution reverts to the 1959 pattern and is similar for males and fe-

TABLE 4.3

Percentage Distribution of Arrests by Social Class and Sex, Controlling for Year

	Social Class			
			Total	
	Lower	Higher	Percent	Number
1959				
Male	60.9	39.1	79.4	220
Female	70.2	29.8	20.6	57
Total percent	62.8	37.2		
Total number	174	103		
1969				
Male	63.2	36.8	49.2	193
Female	58.3	41.7	50.8	199
Total percent	60.7	39.3		
Total number	238	154		
1976				
Male	80.6	19.4	47.4	175
Female	83.0	17.0	52.6	194
Total percent	81.8	18.2		
Total number	302	67		

Note: For 1959 x^2 = 1.19113 and p = .255; for 1969 x^2 = .79911 and p = .371; for 1976 x^2 = .21762 and p = .6409.

Source: Compiled by the author.

males. Most female offenders are from the lower social classes (83 percent), as are most male offenders (80 percent).

Race and Social Class Interaction

Sex role theorists predict that sex role changes are likely to affect middle-class, white females more strongly than any other group. Therefore, the racial and social class distribution of female offenders in 1959, 1969, and 1976 are of special interest. In Table 4.4 we see, as predicted, a rise in the percentage of arrests among higher-social-class, white offenders in 1969. The percentage of higher-social-class, white offenders is higher in 1969 (40.2 percent) than in 1959 (21.1 percent) but is much lower in 1976 (12.1 percent). Whatever caused the rise in offenders in this group in 1969 was not repeated or did not have the same effect in 1976.

In contrast, the distribution by race and social class of male offenders, displayed in Table 4.5, indicates over time an increase in the percentage of lower-class, black offenders and a decrease in higher-class, white offenders. The social class distribution in 1969 of male offenders was consistent with this trend. The distribution of female offenders in 1969, only, is unique.

TABLE 4.4

Percentage Distribution of Female Arrests by Year, Social Class, and Race

| | Year | | |
	1959	1969	1976
Lower-class blacks	35.1	23.6	49.5
Lower-class whites	35.1	34.7	33.7
Higher-class blacks	8.8	1.5	4.7
Higher-class whites	21.1	40.2	12.1
Total percent	100	100	100
Total number	57	199	190

Source: Compiled by the author.

TABLE 4.5

Percentage Distribution of Male Arrests by Year, Social Class, and Race

| | Year | | |
	1959	1969	1976
Lower-class blacks	25.6	32.1	46.9
Lower-class whites	35.2	31.1	33.7
Higher-class blacks	3.7	4.1	8.6
Higher-class whites	35.6	32.6	10.9
Total percent	100	100	100
Total number	219	193	175

Source: Compiled by the author.

First Offenders

Sex role theory implies that as women's positions in the world change more women will be likely to experiment with illegal activity, either because of a new self-image (Adler 1975) or new opportunities (Simon 1975) or both. Therefore, the ratio of first offenders to repeat offenders would be expected to be especially high in 1969 and 1976. Table 4.6 indicates this was not the case. Female arrests

TABLE 4.6

Prior Criminal Record by Year, Female Arrests
(in percent)

| | Year | | | | |
	1939	1949	1959	1969	1976
First offenders	76.0	83.3	68.3	75.2	50.8
Repeat offenders	24.0	16.7	31.7	24.8	49.2
Total percent	100	100	100	100	100
Total number	25	24	63	210	197

Note: $x^2 = 32.56342$, $p = .00000$, $\gamma = .355$.

Source: Compiled by the author.

TABLE 4.7

Prior Criminal Record by Year, Male Arrests
(in percent)

	Year				
	1939	1949	1959	1969	1976
First offenders	36.4	39.3	50.4	57.5	43.8
Repeat offenders	63.6	60.7	49.6	42.5	56.2
Total percent	100	100	100	100	100
Total number	187	333	234	200	178

Note: $x^2 = 25.45126$, p = .0000; $\gamma = -.14906$.

Source: Compiled by the author.

generally include a high number of first offenders, and arrests in 1969 are not unusual in this respect. In fact, 1976 arrests are unusual in that there is a noticeably smaller percentage of first offenders.

The pattern for males (see Table 4.7) shows an increasing percentage of first offenders over time, except for a reversal in this pattern in 1976. Thus, for males, too, 1969 arrests included a large percentage of first offenders.

TRENDS IN THE SERIOUSNESS OF OFFENSES

Comparison of Male and Female Offenses over Time

What has almost become a truism in criminology—that men commit more serious offenses than women—appears to be a consistent phenomenon in Metroville only in the later years sampled. In 1969 (Table 4.9) and 1976 (Table 4.10), men are more likely than women to be arrested for the more serious property offenses and crimes against people. In 1959 (Table 4.8), however, the picture is more muddled: a higher percentage of women than men are arrested for the less serious property and the most serious property and personal crimes. Arrests in 1949 showed the expected correlation between sex and seriousness, although in 1939 arrests for more serious offenses are more likely to be of females than males.

An analysis of male offenses from 1939 to 1976 (Table 4.11) confirms the generally held notion that there has been an increase

TABLE 4.8

Percentage Distribution of Offense Seriousness of Arrests by Sex,
1959

Offense Seriousness*	Sex	
	Male	Female
Victimless		
(3.53)	58.1	44.4
Property I		
(5.14-5.67)	20.5	38.1
Property II and Personal I		
(6.21-6.57)	18.8	11.1
Most serious property and personal		
(6.97-7.37)	2.6	6.3
Total percent	100	100
Total number	234	63

*See Table 2.2, Rossi's Seriousness Scores for Offenses.

Note: $x^2 = 11.83321$, p = .0000.

Source: Compiled by the author.

TABLE 4.9

Percentage Distribution of Offense Seriousness of Arrests by Sex,
1969

Offense Seriousness*	Sex	
	Male	Female
Victimless		
(3.53)	47.5	57.6
Property I		
(5.14-5.67)	26.5	25.2
Property II and Personal I		
(6.21-6.57)	22.5	16.2
Most serious property and personal		
(6.97-7.37)	3.5	1.0
Total percent	100	100
Total number	200	210

*See Table 2.2, Rossi's Seriousness Scores for Offenses.

Note: $x^2 = 7.19943$, p = .0658.

Source: Compiled by the author.

TABLE 4.10

Percentage Distribution of Offense Seriousness of Arrests by Sex, 1976

	Sex	
Offense Seriousness*	Male	Female
Victimless		
(3.53)	35.4	48.7
Property I		
(5.14-5.67)	33.7	27.9
Property II and Personal I		
(6.21-6.57)	25.3	19.8
Most serious property and personal		
(6.97-7.37)	5.6	3.6
Total percent	100	100
Total number	178	197

*See Table 2.2, Rossi's Seriousness Scores for Offenses.

Note: $x^2 = 7.07993$, p = .0694.

Source: Compiled by the author.

over time in the seriousness of offenses committed. The data of Table 4.12 indicate that this is true for females also, with a few exceptions. Metroville in 1969 saw a noticeable increase in arrests for fraud and forgery and for drugs, which reflects national trends noted by others (Hansen 1975; Simon 1975). This upward trend, however, did not continue in 1976. Interestingly, the percentage of simple assaults is high in 1969 and 1976, as it is in 1939. 1959 is unusual in that there is a high percentage of aggravated assaults. In sum, there is a clear pattern in the male data but mixed trends in the female data. In order to clarify empirical trends, controls were introduced on social class, race, and age.

Controlling for Social Class

With controls for social class, it becomes apparent that for men there is no statistically significant difference in seriousness of arrests between the social classes (Table 4.13). There is, however, a statistically significant difference in arrests between females of lower and higher social classes in 1969. As one sees in Table 4.14, higher-class females are more likely than lower-class females to be arrested for fraud and forgery and drugs. This pattern is not evi-

TABLE 4.11

Percentage Distribution of Seriousness of Offense of Arrests by
Year, Males

Offense Seriousness*	Year				
	1939	1949	1959	1969	1976
3.53	85.6	85.7	58.1	47.5	35.4
5.14	2.7	2.4	15.4	14.5	15.2
5.45	0.0	0.0	1.3	0.5	1.7
5.62	0.0	0.0	0.9	4.5	2.8
5.67	0.0	3.0	3.0	7.0	14.0
6.21	2.1	2.1	4.7	7.5	7.9
6.57	7.0	4.2	14.1	15.0	17.4
6.97	0.0	0.0	0.0	0.0	1.1
7.18	2.7	0.9	2.1	2.5	1.7
7.33	0.0	0.0	0.4	0.5	2.8
7.37	0.0	0.3	0.0	0.5	0.0
Total percent	100	100	100	100	100
Total number	187	333	234	200	178

*See Table 2.2, Rossi's Seriousness Scores for Offenses.

Note: $x^2 = 273.71265$, p = .0000.

Source: Compiled by the author.

denced in the 1959 data, but is consistent with 1976 female data.
While simple assaults are predominantly a lower-class female offense in 1959, 1969, and 1976, higher-class females in 1969 are more
likely to be arrested for assaults on police officers than lower-class
females.

Controlling for Race

Among men, there has been little consistent difference between
the seriousness of black and white arrests (see Tables 4.15, 4.16,
and 4.17). Only in 1959 is there a statistically significant difference
between races, with blacks being arrested for more serious offenses
than whites (Table 4.16).

Among females, there is a statistically significant difference
in arrests of blacks and whites in 1959, 1969, and 1976. In 1959 and
1976, black arrests are for more serious offenses than white arrests

TABLE 4.12

Percentage Distribution of Seriousness of Offense of Arrests by
Year, Females

| Offense | Year | | | | |
Seriousness*	1939	1949	1959	1969	1976
3.53					
(victimless)	60.0	87.5	44.4	57.6	48.7
5.14	12.0	4.2	33.3	6.2	12.7
5.45	4.0	0.0	0.0	0.5	4.6
5.62					
(drugs)	0.0	0.0	1.6	5.2	2.0
5.67					
(fraud and forgery)	8.0	4.2	3.2	13.3	8.6
6.21	0.0	0.0	3.2	0.5	2.0
6.39	0.0	0.0	0.0	0.0	0.5
6.57					
(assault)	16.0	4.2	7.9	15.7	17.3
6.97					
(assault on police					
officer)	0.0	0.0	1.6	0.5	1.5
7.18					
(aggravated assault)	0.0	0.0	0.0	0.5	2.0
Total percent	100	100	100	100	100
Total number	25	24	63	210	197

*See Table 2.2, Rossi's Serious Scores for Offenses.

Note: x^2 = 80.76466, p = .0000.

Source: Compiled by the author.

(compare Tables 4.18 and 4.19). In 1969 this pattern is interrupted
only by the higher percentage of white arrests for drugs, fraud and
forgery, and most serious property offenses (Table 4.18). Note that
this is not true in 1976 (Table 4.19).

To summarize the data thus far: sex role theory predicts that
changes brought on by the women's movement will produce a "new
female criminal," who will be white, of a higher social class, and
probably a first offender. The data support this hypothesis. However, this is true only in 1969, not 1976. That is, the data show a
greater percentage of higher-social-class, white, and first offenders
in 1969 compared with 1959. In 1976, however, higher-social-class,

TABLE 4.13

Seriousness of Offense by Social Class Controlling for Year, Male Arrests
(in percent)

Offense Seriousness*	1959 Low	1959 High	1969 Low	1969 High	1976 Low	1976 High
3.53	55.2	62.8	41.8	56.3	34.8	38.2
5.14	14.2	15.1	17.2	9.9	16.3	8.8
5.45	0.7	2.3	0.0	1.4	1.4	2.9
5.62						
(drugs)	1.5	0.0	4.9	4.2	2.8	2.9
5.67						
(fraud and forgery)	2.2	3.5	7.4	5.6	12.8	20.6
6.21	6.7	1.2	6.6	8.5	7.1	11.8
6.57						
(assault)	14.9	15.1	18.0	11.3	18.4	11.8
7.18	3.7	0.0	3.3	1.4	2.1	0.0
7.33	0.7	0.0	0.0	1.4	2.8	2.9
7.37	0.0	0.0	0.8	0.0	0.0	0.0
Total percent	100	100	100	100	100	100
Total number	134	86	122	71	141	34

*See Table 2.2, Rossi's Seriousness Scores for Offenses.

Note: For 1959 x^2 = 10.49504, p = .2320, γ = -.16041; for 1969 x^2 = 10.10039, p = .3424, γ = -.20006; for 1976 x^2 = 5.55905, p = .8038, γ = -.06303.

Source: Compiled by the author.

TABLE 4.14

Seriousness of Offense by Social Class Controlling for Year, Female Arrests
(in percent)

Offense Seriousness*	1959		1969		1976	
	Low	High	Low	High	Low	High
3.53	50.0	35.3	56.0	59.0	48.4	48.5
5.14	25.0	47.1	5.2	6.0	10.6	21.2
5.45	0.0	0.0	0.9	0.0	5.0	3.0
5.62 (drugs)	2.5	0.0	4.3	7.2	1.2	6.1
5.67 (fraud and forgery)	2.5	0.0	8.6	19.3	8.1	12.1
6.21	5.0	0.0	0.9	0.0	2.5	0.0
6.39	0.0	0.0	0.0	0.0	0.0	3.0
6.57 (assault)	10.0	5.9	23.3	7.2	19.9	6.1
6.97 (assault on police officer)	0.0	5.9	0.0	1.2	1.9	0.0
7.18	5.0	5.9	0.9	0.0	2.5	0.0
Total percent	100	100	100	100	100	100
Total number	40	17	116	83	161	33

*See Table 2.2, Rossi's Seriousness Scores for Offenses.

Note: For 1959 $x^2 = 6.7052$, $p = .4602$, $\gamma = .13924$; for 1969 $x^2 = 16.14735$, $p = .0403$, $\gamma = -.13150$; for 1976 $x^2 = 16.44565$, $p = .0581$, $\gamma = -.14458$.

Source: Compiled by the author.

TABLE 4.15

Seriousness of Offense by Race for Males in 1939 and 1949
(in percent)

Offense	1939		1949	
Seriousness*	Black	White	Black	White
3.53	81.3	87.1	84.9	87.9
5.14	2.1	2.9	2.2	2.5
5.67	0.0	0.0	3.2	2.9
6.21	4.2	1.4	2.2	2.1
6.57	6.3	7.2	5.4	3.8
7.18	6.3	1.4	2.2	0.4
7.37	0.0	0.0	0.0	0.4
Total percent	100	100	100	100
Total number	48	139	93	239

*See Table 2.2, Rossi's Seriousness Scores for Offenses.

Note: For 1939 $x^2 = 4.60018$, $p = .3308$; for 1949 $x^2 = 3.14613$, $p = .7903$.

Source: Compiled by the author.

TABLE 4.16

Seriousness of Offense by Race for Males in 1959 and 1969
(in percent)

Offense	1959		1969	
Seriousness*	Black	White	Black	White
3.53	45.6	63.2	43.1	50.0
5.14	16.2	14.7	15.3	14.1
5.45	0.0	1.8	0.0	0.8
5.62	1.5	0.6	5.6	3.9
5.67	4.4	2.5	6.9	7.0
6.21	4.4	4.9	5.6	8.6
6.57	20.6	11.7	19.4	12.5
7.18	7.4	0.0	2.8	2.3
7.33	0.0	0.6	0.0	0.8
7.37	0.0	0.0	1.4	0.0
Total percent	100	100	100	100
Total number	68	163	72	128

*See Table 2.2, Rossi's Seriousness Scores for Offenses.

Note: For 1959 $x^2 = 20.00195$, $p = .0103$; for 1969 $x^2 = 5.77992$, $p = .7617$.

Source: Compiled by the author.

TABLE 4.17

Seriousness of Offense by Race for Males in 1976
(in percent)

Offense Seriousness*	Race	
	Black	White
3.53	26.5	46.3
5.14	16.3	13.8
5.45	1.0	2.5
5.62	1.0	5.0
5.67	17.3	10.0
6.21	9.2	6.3
6.57	19.4	15.0
6.97	2.0	0.0
7.18	3.1	0.0
7.33	4.1	1.3
Total percent	100	100
Total number	98	80

*See Table 2.2, Rossi's Seriousness Scores for Offenses.

Note: $x^2 = 16.08766$, p = .0651.

Source: Compiled by the author.

white, first offenders are not dominating the arrest statistics. In fact, the 1976 offender clearly resembles the 1969 offender in social class, race, and type of offense. If the women's movement and change in sex roles and in opportunities were the etiological factors in 1969, why did they not continue to have an impact in 1976?

The next step is to examine the frequency-of-offense data by age to see if new patterns emerge.

Controlling for Age

Same-Sex Comparisons over Time

Computation of a rank order correlation coefficient (r_s) for juvenile and adult arrests separately introduces a new perspective on the data. A comparison of Spearman correlation coefficients for male and female adults separately (Table 4.20) shows that over time the rank ordering of adult female offenses is most different between 1949 and 1959 (.37). There is less variation in the most frequent offenses committed by females between other periods—even between 1959 and 1976 (.56)—than there is between 1949 and 1959. Note there is not a unique change in the rank ordering of female adult offenses between 1959 and 1969.

The pattern for male adults is quite different. Here we see little variation in the rank ordering of offenses between adjacent periods. Moreover, consistent with a steady trend of increasing seriousness of arrests, the greatest difference between periods is in the comparative ranking of offenses in 1959 and in 1976 (.25). Note this is not true for females.

TABLE 4.18

Seriousness of Offense by Race for Females in 1959 and 1969
(by percent)

Offense Seriousness*	1959		1969	
	Black	White	Black	White
3.53	61.5	32.4	48.0	60.6
5.14	11.5	48.6	4.0	6.9
5.45	0.0	0.0	0.0	0.6
5.62 (drugs)	0.0	2.7	0.0	6.9
5.67 (fraud and forgery)	0.0	5.4	6.0	15.6
6.21 (larceny over $200, burglary, auto theft)	3.8	2.7	0.0	0.6
6.57 (assault)	11.5	5.4	38.0	8.8
6.97	0.0	2.7	2.0	0.0
7.18	11.5	0.0	2.0	0.0
Total percent	100	100	100	100
Total number	26	37	50	160

*See Table 2.2, Rossi's Seriousness Scores for Offenses.

Note: For 1959 x^2 = 17.08595, p = .0169; for 1969 x^2 = 35.41272, p = .0000.

Source: Compiled by the author.

TABLE 4.19

Seriousness of Offense by Race for Females in 1976
(in percent)

Offense Seriousness*	Race	
	Black	White
3.53	35.6	64.0
5.14	15.4	10.1
5.45	3.8	4.5
5.62	1.0	3.4
5.67	13.5	3.4
6.21	2.9	1.1
6.39	0.0	1.1
6.57	22.1	11.2
6.97	1.9	1.1
7.18	3.8	0.0
Total percent	100	100
Total number	104	89

*See Table 2.2, Rossi's Seriousness Scores for Offenses.

Note: x^2 = 24.77124, p = .0032.

Source: Compiled by the author.

For juveniles, the story is slightly different (see Table 4.21). Relative to other periods, there is more dissimilarity in the ranking of female juvenile offenses between 1959 and 1969 (.10), although, once again, the most frequent female offenses in 1959 are similar to those in 1976 (.42). For males, the greatest change in the kinds of offenses most likely to be committed occurred between 1949 and 1959 (.21). From then on, male juvenile arrests show a similar distribution over time, even comparing 1959 and 1976 arrests.

Male-Female Comparisons over Time

The Spearman correlation comparing adult male and female arrests (Table 4.22) shows more disparity between the frequency rank ordering in 1969 (.37) than in any other period. Note this is not true for juveniles (Table 4.23). In 1969 there is more similarity between male and female juvenile arrests (.69) than in periods before or after. In 1959 this pattern is reversed. The rank ordering of male and female adult arrests then is more similar (.65) than in

TABLE 4.20

Spearman Rank Order Correlation Coefficients for Adults

	1939–49	1949–59	1959–69	1969–76	1959–76
Females					
r_s =	.56	.37	.55	.51	.56
N =	36	36	36	36	36
p =	.002	.02	.002	.002	.002
Males					
r_s =	.68	.68	.59	.56	.25
N =	36	36	36	36	36
p =	.002	.002	.002	.002	.14

Source: Compiled by the author.

TABLE 4.21

Spearman Rank Order Correlation Coefficients for Juveniles

	1939–49	1949–59	1959–69	1969–76	1959–76
Females					
r_s =	—	.31	.10	.48	.42
N =	—	34	34	34	34
p =	—	.06	.40	.004	.01
Males					
r_s =	—	.21	.42	.52	.57
N =	—	34	34	34	34
p =	—	.24	.01	.002	.002

Source: Compiled by the author.

TABLE 4.22

Spearman Rank Order Correlation Coefficients Comparing Male and Female Arrests in Specified Years, Adults

	1939	1949	1959	1969	1976
Male-female					
r_s =	.58	.59	.65	.37	.54
N =	36	36	36	36	36
p =	.002	.002	.002	.02	.002

Source: Compiled by the author.

TABLE 4.23

Spearman Rank Order Correlation Coefficients Comparing Male and Female Arrests in Specific Years, Juveniles

	1939	1949	1959	1969	1976
Male-female					
r_s =	—	.41	.35	.69	.45
N =	—	34	34	34	34
p =	—	.01	.04	.002	.01

Source: Compiled by the author.

other periods; male and female juvenile arrests are more dissimilar
(.35) than in other periods.

Sex role theorists would predict that females and males, as a
result of the women's movement, are now committing similar crimes.
This seems to be true only for juveniles in 1969. By 1976 the rank
order correlation of male and female juvenile offenses has returned
to its 1959 pattern. To explore further the change in juvenile activity
in 1969, the effect of friendship patterns on offense activity will be
examined.

FRIENDSHIP NETWORKS

Peer networks have been of theoretical interest because it has
been posited that "the repeater tends to be a member of a regular
group" (Wattenberg 1957) and that cross-sex friendship patterns affect delinquency (Giordano 1974; Pollak 1950).

The social context in which much delinquency occurs has been
noted by many. The importance of same-sex "age mates" in encour-
aging delinquency has led to extensive empirical research on gang
delinquency and the more general "group process" (Bordua 1961;
Cloward and Ohlin 1960; Cohen 1955; Cohen and Short 1958; Hood and
Sparks 1970; Miller 1958; Short 1968; Short and Strodtbeck 1965; Wattenberg 1957; Yablonsky 1967).

The classical literature emphasizes the masculine nature of
the subcultures that exert an antisocial influence on adolescents.
The assumption is that female friendship networks do not exert this
type of influence on their members (Barker and Adams 1962; Reckless 1957). Miller (1973) observed recently that "the girls have the
same opportunities to follow the same pursuits and to commit the
same crimes that boys do, but that their most frequent offense was
truancy" (p. 35).

Coleman's (1961) research noted the proliferation of extensive
cliques or gangs within the youth culture. Peer relations among girls
were thought to be as tightly knit and complex as those among boys.
While Coleman does not document criminal activity, he does report
cliques or gangs of girls who were known to be "fast" or "tough"—
girls who reported smoking, drinking, or "hanging around the skating
rink." Others, while concentrating on male gang activities, provide
impressionistic evidence of autonomous peer activity on the part of
girls as well (David 1972, Suttles 1968). The quality of female friendship networks is suggested in studies of incarcerated females who report membership in a gang (Giallombardo 1974; Giordano 1974). These
studies suggest the potentially volatile nature of female peer relations.

The effect of females on male delinquency has also been a source
of controversy. Pollak's thesis that women goad men into crimes has

TABLE 4.24

Extent of Companionship in Juvenile Arrests by Sex, 1959
(in percent)

Number of	Sex	
Companions	Male	Female
None	11.7	50.0
One	23.3	25.0
Two or more	65.0	25.0
Total percent	100	100
Total number	60	24

Note: x^2 = 16.27682, p = .0003.
Source: Compiled by the author.

TABLE 4.25

Extent of Companionship in Juvenile Arrests by Sex, 1969
(in percent)

Number of	Sex	
Companions	Male	Female
None	29.1	21.9
One	30.1	37.5
Two or more	40.8	40.6
Total percent	100	100
Total number	103	128

Note: x^2 = 2.11011, p = .3482.
Source: Compiled by the author.

TABLE 4.26

Extent of Companionship in Juvenile Arrests by Sex, 1976
(in percent)

Number of	Sex	
Companions	Male	Female
None	40.9	57.0
One	29.6	24.6
Two or more	29.6	18.3
Total percent	100	100
Total number	115	142

Note: x^2 = 7.35704, p = .0253.
Source: Compiled by the author.

been disputed in the Klein and Luce (1971) study of half a dozen gangs of black girls and their influence on boys' gang activities. They found that girls seldom participated in or helped to plan the boys' gang activities and that on the contrary, their presence often postponed or ended illicit activities planned by the boys. Other studies emphasized the traditional helpmate role that girls have played in male gangs (Horowitz and Schwartz 1974; Thomas 1967; Whyte 1955).

The extent and effect of mixed-sex groups is of interest because of the impact that sex role changes may be expected to have on friendship networks. Are gangs now more likely to be egalitarian? Is the seriousness of a group's criminal activity affected by its sex composition? While these data provide no evidence of gang formations, an examination of the group process is possible. Sex composition and its effect on a group's delinquent activity can be analyzed.

It is interesting to note that from the data of Tables 4.24, 4.25, and 4.26 it is clear that the traditional companionship pattern established in the 1959 data is broken in 1969 and then reestablished in 1976. That is, in 1959 there is a statistically significant correlation between sex and the likelihood of companions in offense activity. Males are more likely than females to have companions (to be with a group of at least two others) when arrested for an offense (Table

TABLE 4.27

Seriousness of Offense by Sex Composition of Juvenile Groups
Arrested, 1959
(in percent)

| Offense | Sex Composition | | |
Seriousness*	All Male	All Female	Mixed Sex
3.53	37.9	22.2	66.7
5.14	43.1	77.8	0.0
5.45	3.4	0.0	0.0
5.67	3.4	0.0	0.0
6.21	6.9	0.0	0.0
6.57	1.7	0.0	0.0
6.97	0.0	0.0	33.3
7.18	3.4	0.0	0.0
Total percent	100	100	100
Total number	58	9	3

*See Table 2.2, Rossi's Seriousness Scores for Offenses.

Note: $x^2 = 29.34424$, p = .0094.

Source: Compiled by the author.

4.24). In 1969 this pattern disappears. Girls and boys show similar propensities to be with a group when an arrest is made (Table 4.25). In 1976 the pattern reverses to that of 1959 (Table 4.26).

When comparing the effect of group composition on crime seriousness, a similar trend emerges. In 1959 all-female groups commit the least serious offenses; all-male groups, the most serious; and mixed group is erratic (Table 4.27). In 1969 this picture is reversed. All-female groups are committing more serious offenses than formerly and are competitive with male groups in terms of crime seriousness. Mixed groups are less serious offenders than either same-sex group (Table 4.28).

In 1976 female groups are not as aggressive as all-male groups. Mixed groups are more varied in their activity than in 1959 and along with all-male groups commit the more serious offenses (Table 4.29). In this data, we find the 1959 picture has been reestablished, but with some modifications. All-female groups in 1976 are as traditional as they were in 1959, but mixed groups are more likely to be volatile and untraditional in their pursuits.

While there is a tendency for whites to commit offenses in a group, there is no statistically significant correlation between race and likelihood to have companions for either sex in 1969 or 1976. The propensity to commit offenses with a friend is not a racial trait. Turning from juvenile activity, our focus shifts to an examination of the professionalism-versus-socialization hypothesis.

TABLE 4.28

Seriousness of Offense by Sex Composition of Juvenile Groups
Arrested, 1969
(in percent)

Offense Seriousness*	Sex Composition		
	All Male	All Female	Mixed Sex
3.53	38.7	51.8	66.0
5.14	24.2	1.8	5.7
5.62	4.8	8.9	5.7
5.67	6.5	21.4	17.0
6.21	9.7	0.0	0.0
6.57	16.1	16.1	5.7
Total percent	100	100	100
Total number	62	56	53

*See Table 2.2, Rossi's Seriousness Scores for Offenses.

Note: $x^2 = 38.7894$, p = .000.

Source: Compiled by the author.

TABLE 4.29

Seriousness of Offense by Sex Composition of Juvenile Groups
Arrested, 1976
(in percent)

| Offense | Sex Composition | | |
Seriousness*	All Male	All Female	Mixed Sex
3.53	29.5	61.5	39.4
5.14	21.3	11.5	12.1
5.45	1.6	3.8	3.0
5.62	3.3	0.0	3.0
5.67	16.4	7.7	9.1
6.21	6.6	0.0	23.1
6.57	18.0	15.4	21.2
6.97	1.6	0.0	0.0
7.33	1.6	0.0	0.0
Total percent	100	100	100
Total number	61	26	33

*See Table 2.2, Rossi's Seriousness Scores for Offenses.

Note: $x^2 = 14.57052$, p = .5563.

Source: Compiled by the author.

PROFESSIONALISM VERSUS SOCIALIZATION

In order to examine the source of the alleged aggressiveness
of the new female criminal, several hypotheses concerning first offenders are suggested in Chapter 1. Specifically, sex role theory
predicts that changes in sex role definitions will lead over time to:
(1) increasing seriousness of offense of first offenders, (2) commission of first offense at an earlier age, and (3) more serious offenses
of younger offenders compared with older offenders. For the third
hypothesis, it is necessary to control for criminal experience. This
will be done by testing the hypothesis on first offenders only. These
hypotheses attempt to refute the proposition that seriousness of offense is increasing due to the activity of experienced (that is, chronic)
offenders. This has been termed the "professionalism" theory.

Seriousness of Offense of First Offenders

Careful consideration of Tables 4.30 and 4.31 show generally
an increasing seriousness of offense of first offenders, male or fe-

TABLE 4.30

Seriousness of Offense by Year, Male First Offenders
(in percent)

| Offense | Year | | | | |
Seriousness*	1939	1949	1959	1969	1976
Victimless					
(3.53)	80.9	81.7	59.3	50.4	34.6
Drugs					
(5.62)	0.0	0.0	0.0	2.6	1.3
Property I					
(5.14, 5.67)	4.4	9.2	25.4	21.7	25.6
Property II					
(6.21, 6.39, 7.33)	4.4	3.8	2.5	7.8	9.0
Personal I					
(6.57)	8.8	3.8	9.3	15.7	25.6
Personal II					
(6.97, 7.12, 7.18, 7.37)	1.5	1.5	2.5	1.7	2.6
Other					
(5.45)	0.0	0.0	0.8	0.0	1.3
Total percent	100	100	100	100	100
Total number	68	131	118	115	78

*See Table 2.2, Rossi's Seriousness Scores for Offenses.

Note: $x^2 = 83.85944$, $p = .0000$.

Source: Compiled by the author.

male. However, the pattern of steadily increasing seriousness is interrupted by unusually high percentages, for both men and women, of less serious property crimes (Property I) and more serious personal crimes (Personal II) in 1959. Whatever precipitated this rise cannot be sex role specific, since both males and females are affected.

In analyzing Tables 4.32 and 4.33, it is clear that the pattern is the same for black and white females: both show a higher percentage of less serious property offenses (5.14) in 1959. It is interesting to note that in 1969 drugs (5.62) are entirely a white female offense and that the rise in fraud and forgery and undefined larceny (5.67) in 1969 is due to the activity of white, not black, female first offenders. In 1976 this activity drops off among whites and is picked up by black, female first offenders. Conversely, the high percentage of assaults

(6.57) in 1969 is due to the activity of black females; in 1976 there is, however, an increase in the percentage of assaults among white first offenders.

Age at First Offense

Sex role theory predicts commission of first offense at an earlier age as sex role changes loosen social controls and modify socialization practices. A comparison of Tables 4.34 and 4.35 indicates the pattern for males and females is generally the same. Table 4.34 considers males. First offenders are older in 1939 and 1949—the modal age category then is 25-34. In 1959 first offenders are not predominantly from any age group. By 1969 the spread evidenced in 1959 has disappeared and, now, first offenders are concentrated in

TABLE 4.31

Seriousness of Offense by Year, Female First Offenders
(in percent)

Offense	Year				
Seriousness*	1939	1949	1959	1969	1976
Victimless					
(3.53)	52.6	90.0	34.9	53.8	41.0
Drugs					
(5.62)	0.0	0.0	0.0	5.7	2.0
Property I					
(5.14, 5.67)	21.1	10.0	41.9	23.4	28.0
Property II					
(6.21, 6.39, 7.33)	0.0	0.0	2.3	0.0	3.0
Personal I					
(6.57)	21.1	0.0	11.6	15.8	19.0
Personal II					
(6.97, 7.12, 7.18, 7.37)	0.0	0.0	9.3	0.6	3.0
Other	5.3	0.0	0.0	0.6	4.0
Total percent	100	100	100	100	100
Total number	19	20	43	153	100

*See Table 2.2, Rossi's Seriousness Scores for Offenses.

Note: $x^2 = 52.03125$; $p = .0008$.

Source: Compiled by the author.

TABLE 4.32

Seriousness of Offense by Year, Female Black First Offenders
(in percent)

Offense	Year				
Seriousness*	1939	1949	1959	1969	1976
Victimless					
(3.53)	33.3	100.0	50.0	34.5	33.3
Property I					
(5.14)	33.3	0.0	7.1	3.4	18.3
Property I					
(5.67)	11.1	0.0	0.0	6.9	18.3
Property II					
(6.21)	0.0	0.0	0.0	0.0	1.7
Personal I					
(6.57)	22.2	0.0	21.4	51.7	23.3
Personal II					
(6.97)	0.0	0.0	0.0	0.0	1.7
Personal II					
(7.18)	0.0	0.0	21.4	3.4	1.7
Other					
(5.45)	0.0	0.0	0.0	0.0	1.7
Total percent	100	100	100	100	100
Total number	9	11	14	29	60

*See Table 2.2, Rossi's Seriousness Scores for Offenses.

Note: x^2 = 49.72928, p = .0069.

Source: Compiled by the author.

the younger age groups—the modal age category is 15-17. In 1976 the median age category is 15-17 and the modal category is 11-14— the 1969 pattern is sustained in 1976.

For females (Table 4.35) the male pattern is repeated, except that the jump to the younger age categories—so evident among males in 1969—for females, takes place in 1959. In 1959, 1969, and 1976, the modal and median age category is 15-17 years.

For males and females, the picture is not altered by examining blacks and whites separately. Indeed, among females, the 1959 shift of first offenders to the younger age categories is more dramatic for white females than for black females.

TABLE 4.33

Seriousness of Offense by Year, Female White First Offenders
(in percent)

Offense	Year				
Seriousness*	1939	1949	1959	1969	1976
Victimless					
(3.53)	70.0	75.0	27.6	58.1	53.8
Property I					
(5.14)	0.0	12.5	51.7	7.0	10.3
Property I					
(5.67)	0.0	12.5	6.9	19.4	5.1
Drugs					
(5.62)	0.0	0.0	0.0	7.0	5.1
Property II					
(6.21)	0.0	0.0	3.4	0.0	2.6
Property II					
(6.39)	0.0	0.0	0.0	0.0	2.6
Personal I					
(6.57)	20.0	0.0	6.9	7.8	12.8
Personal II					
(6.97)	0.0	0.0	3.4	0.0	2.6
Other					
(5.45)	10.0	0.0	0.0	0.8	5.1
Total percent	100	100	100	100	100
Total number	10	8	29	129	39

*See Table 2.2, Rossi's Seriousness Scores for Offenses.

Note: x^2 = 76.85587, p = .0000.

Source: Compiled by the author.

Comparison of Seriousness of Offense
of Young and Old Offenders

Among first offenders, sex role changes have not led to more
serious offenses being committed by younger offenders compared with
older offenders. Comparing 1959, 1969, and 1976, it appears that
one pattern prevails: for women first offenders, younger people tend
to commit a larger percentage of the less serious offenses than do
older people. This pattern, which is not changed in 1969 or 1976,

TABLE 4.34

Age of First Offenders by Year, Males
(in percent)

Age	Year				
(years)	1939	1949	1959	1969	1976
6–10	0.0	0.0	3.5	7.0	9.0
11–14	0.0	0.8	17.4	30.7	32.1
15–17	3.0	4.7	16.5	43.0	25.6
18–24	25.8	17.1	17.4	8.8	12.8
25–34	33.3	26.4	13.9	6.1	7.7
35–44	12.1	22.5	16.5	2.6	5.1
45–54	15.2	14.7	7.8	0.9	5.1
55–76	10.6	14.0	7.0	0.9	2.6
Total percent	100	100	100	100	100
Total number	66	126	115	114	78

Note: x^2 = 231.78897, p = .000.

Source: Compiled by the author.

TABLE 4.35

Age of First Offenders by Year, Females
(in percent)

Age	Year				
(years)	1939	1949	1959	1969	1976
6–10	0.0	0.0	0.0	5.1	6.0
11–14	0.0	5.6	16.7	22.2	23.0
15–17	5.3	0.0	35.7	55.7	28.0
18–24	31.6	22.2	7.1	5.7	21.0
25–34	31.6	38.9	11.9	6.3	15.0
35–44	15.8	16.7	23.8	1.9	5.0
45–54	5.3	16.7	2.4	3.2	0.0
55–76	10.5	0.0	2.4	0.0	2.0
Total percent	100	100	100	100	100
Total number	19	18	42	158	100

Note: x^2 = 133.39545, p = .0000.

Source: Compiled by the author.

has been noted in more general discussions of female criminality (Gibbons 1977; Sutherland and Cressey 1978).

Among males the reverse pattern is expected (Sutherland and Cressey 1978) and is to be found in these data. That is, there is among male first offenders a tendency for juvenile offenders to commit more serious offenses than adult offenders.

In addition, in support of the professionalism hypothesis, it should be noted that the age at first offense of those female, repeat offenders arrested in 1969 and 1976 is significantly lower than the median or modal age of first offense of those female repeat offenders arrested in 1939, 1949, or 1959. Thus, female repeat offenders in 1969 and 1976 started their criminal careers at an earlier age than in other periods, and in this sense can be considered more experienced.

CONCLUSION

From Table 3.3 in Chapter 3, it is clear that arrests of juvenile female offenders are increasing at a greater pace than those of adult female offenders. In this chapter, we find the predicted rise in female arrests of white offenders, higher-class offenders, and white, higher-class, juvenile offenders. This picture, which is supportive of sex role theory, is marred by the fact that this condition, established in 1969, is not continued in 1976. Rather, it is reversed and there is a return to the pattern established earlier.

In 1969 Metroville experienced a marked increase in arrests of white higher-class offenders for drugs, fraud and forgery, and the more serious property offenses. This reflects national trends. Moreover, while assaults are predominantly a lower-class offense among females, in 1969 higher-class females were more likely to be arrested for assaults on police officers than lower-class females. However, there was not a similar pattern of offense seriousness among higher-class white offenders in 1976. An explanation in terms of sex role changes would have to explain why the 1969 pattern is not maintained in 1976.

To examine the hypothesis that changes in seriousness of offense activity are as likely to be due to increased experience of the chronic offender (professionalism) as they are to be due to changes in the socialization practices or family social controls, the activity of first offenders was analyzed vis-à-vis age and type of criminal offense. The age of first offenders, while low in 1969, first drops markedly among white females in 1959. Moreover, younger first offenders commit less serious offenses than do older first offenders. These data on first offenders do not support sex role predictions. Yet, it is interesting to note that a high percentage of fraud and forgery charges in the 1969 data were due to the activity of young, white first offenders.

It is interesting that the pattern of change in offense activity is different for juvenile and adult females. Female adults experienced the greatest change in the type of offense most likely to be committed between 1949 and 1959; juveniles, between 1959 and 1969. Furthermore, male and female offense activity was most similar among juveniles in 1969; among adults, in 1959. Thus it would seem that social forces in 1969 had their greatest impact on juveniles.

Among juveniles there was a marked increase in the number of arrests of females in 1969 compared to other periods; the rank ordering of male and female juvenile offenses is most similar in 1969; and the rank ordering of female juvenile offenses changed the most from 1959 to 1969. Moreover, the data on sex composition of juvenile groups and also its correlation with offense activity seem to attest to the impact of changing sex roles.

In 1969 girls are as likely as boys to be with a group when an arrest is made. There is some evidence that 1969 was the beginning of a new trend among juveniles and not simply an isolated aberration. All-female groups in 1969 were arrested for more serious offenses than previously. And mixed-sex groups showed an increasing tendency (from 1959 to 1976) to pursue less traditional, more volatile juvenile activity. In 1959, since the predominant activity was drinking, their concerns were presumably the traditional "boy meets girl" variety. By 1976 the seriousness of offense of all female groups is reduced, but the activity of mixed-sex groups is much less traditional and more serious. The role that females play in these groups is, of course, unknown.

The sex role theorists point to the impact of social and cultural forces affecting people's lives, influencing the propensity to commit crime. The women's movement, in particular, has become a focus of attention as an etiological factor in crime. However, it is possible that much of what emerges in these data as increased activity on the part of young (juvenile), white, higher-social-class females is due not to the women's movement but to the activity connected with the antiwar movement, which, like the women's movement, also attracted the attention and energy of the white middle class. If we hypothesize that the antiwar movement is responsible for the "acting out" behavior of females, it becomes easier to explain why the pattern of criminal activity in 1969 is unique and different from that of 1976. The women's movement started around 1969 and continued through 1976. The war and the youthful activity it fomented did not continue into 1976.

Alternatively, it is possible that a change in police personnel and the concomitant likelihood of arrest can also explain this data.

That is, to what extent did the police create the new female juvenile criminal by personnel changes? Since variability in the enforcement of laws is most probable for the less serious offenses, an examination of the percentage of arrests for status offenses and public-order offenses in different periods was conducted.

In 1959, 24 percent of female, juvenile arrests were for status or public-order offenses. However, in 1969, 50 percent of all arrests of juvenile females were for these less serious offenses. In 1976, again, 50 percent of arrests were for status or public-order offenses. Thus, in 1969 and 1976 fully half of all female, juvenile arrests were for these less serious offenses. This is a considerable increase over the percentage of such arrests in 1959. These data seem to suggest that the likelihood of arrest did increase under the new juvenile officer.

The big increase in arrests in 1969 is due in part to the increase in the percentage of runaways (from 4 to 15 percent), which are typically reported by the families, truancy (from 0 to 16 percent), usually reported by the school, and disorderly and drunk-and-disorderly arrests (from 12 to 19 percent). Disorderly, drunk and disorderly, and at times, truancy arrests are more likely to be proactive (Reiss 1971) situations, that is, incidents when the arrest is initiated by police activity rather than in response to citizen complaint. Note that 1969 was a time when juveniles expressed political sentiments (anti-Viet Nam) by "disorderly" behavior that frequently resulted in school absences (truancy). From informal interviews with police officers active in those years, it appears that youth of school age observed in the downtown area during school hours might well have been picked up on a truancy charge. Thus, it is possible that the likelihood of arrest was altered appreciably in the 1960s due to police activity. Of course, one would expect such change in police activity to impact on boys as well as girls. Yet, for boys in 1959, 27 percent of arrests were for status and public-order offenses. This increased to 36 percent in 1969 and dropped down to 24 percent in 1976. While it is possible that the rhetoric of the women's movement affected police perception of female culpability and, therefore, their likelihood of arrest, it is also possible that girls were "acting out" more; their initial acts were ones of truancy and disorderly behavior—a logical place to begin.

Their behavior could have been caused by the rhetoric of the women's movement or by the rhetoric of the antiwar movement. Although we do not know which factor is more important, we do know that the pattern of juvenile behavior in 1976 is not the same as in 1969. Something happened in 1969 that did not continue to have an impact in 1976.

5

TRENDS IN CRIME
SEVERITY EXAMINED BY
COHORT ANALYSIS

INTRODUCTION

Central to the study of social change is an examination of the
way that new birth cohorts* act compared with their predecessors.
Cohort flow is not merely population replacement but the movement
of sequential cohorts, propelled by aging, through age-related and
period-defined roles and institutions. And, as Ryder states, "social
change occurs to the extent that successive cohorts do something other
than merely repeat the patterns of behavior of their predecessors"
(1972, p. 105).

In a diachronic study of society, it is important to understand
the separate impact of three factors: aging, cohort differences, and
period effects. Aging effects are changes due to the normal process
of passing through the inevitable biological life-cycle stages. The individual's stage in the life cycle, determined by the interaction of biological aging with the concomitant passage through a sequence of roles
and institutions, conditions attitudes and actions. For example, Stouffer (1955) researched the relationship between age and tolerance,
questioning the assumption that older people are more resistant to
change than younger people.

Cohort differences refer to the differences between cohorts in
life-course patterns that are a product of either the unique historical

---

*A cohort is customarily defined as "those people within a geo-
graphically or otherwise delineated population who experienced the
same significant life event within a given period of time" (Glenn 1977,
p. 8). The significant life event in this study, as is usually the case,
is birth.

moment through which a cohort passes or its unique demographic characteristics (compare Mannheim 1928, 1952; and Ryder 1965). For
example, environmental factors, such as the state of public health to
which infants are exposed, or time-bound practices by which children
are socialized can produce differences between cohorts. Thus, cohort
differences in political participation and in the incidence of childhood
diseases have been studied (Riley, Johnson, and Foner 1972). Not
only by their unique historical background but also by their size and
sex, race, and ethnic composition are cohorts marked. The cohort
swollen by the baby boom following World War II has been linked to
social changes in educational institutions brought on by the sheer numbers of individuals passing through. For any cohort, the pattern of
aging will reflect the historical background of the cohort and the com-
posite of sociocultural segments that define it.

On the other hand, period effects cut across the age strata and
impact on all segments of society. Long-term changes in income
level, wars, or short-term fluctuations in employment are examples
of period effects that are experienced by all the age strata, though
perhaps in different ways. A study of the suicide rate for white males
shows the period effect of the depression of 1929, which caused rates
to rise irrespective of age (Sainsbury 1963).

The standard cohort table (Glenn 1977) allows an understanding
of the impact of all three factors. That is, in Table 5.1,* looking
down any column one sees a cross-sectional slice at the time of observation. Reading across each row, age-specific comparisons illustrate period effects. The diagonal is a cohort's life cycle, and
the effects of aging are made apparent. By comparing life-cycle patterns of several cohorts (that is, comparing diagonals), cohort differences are highlighted. By comparing a sequence of cohorts one

---

*In Table 5.1 cohorts are defined by their period of birth and
labeled, for convenience, cohort A through K. Note that because the
distance between the last two years of observation (1969 and 1976) is
seven years and not ten as in the other years, two tables (Tables 5.1
and 5.2) were necessary. For the cohort comparisons described on
pp. 89-96 of this chapter, Table 5.1 was used, which maintains the
integrity of the birth years of the cohort. For the period analysis on
pp. 96-103 of this chapter, Table 5.2 was used, which maintains the
age groupings across periods of observation. Essentially, the two
tables are identical except for the last column (labeled 1976). In addition, because in the cohort analysis date of birth was used to group
offenses, and because age was used in the period tables, there is some
slight difference in what presumably would be identical columns in the
two tables.

TABLE 5.1

Key for Defining Cohorts Used in Intracohort Analysis and in
Comparisons of Cohort Differences

Year of Observation				
1939	1949	1959	1969	1976
1922–31 (Cohort A)	1932–41 (Cohort H)	1942–51 (Cohort I)	1952–61 (Cohort J)	1962–71 (Cohort K)
1912–21 (Cohort B)	1922–31	1932–41	1942–51	1952–61
1902–11 (Cohort C)	1912–21	1922–31	1932–41	1942–51
1892–01 (Cohort D)	1902–11	1912–21	1922–31	1932–41
1882–91 (Cohort E)	1892–01	1902–11	1912–21	1922–31
1872–81 (Cohort F)	1882–91	1892–01	1902–11	1912–21
1862–71 (Cohort G)	1872–81	1882–91	1892–01	1902–11

Note: Cells here show year of birth and cohort. In subsequent tables cells will hold information on dependent variable for designated cohorts.

Source: Compiled by the author.

can contrast and explain differences in life-course patterns from one cohort to the next within a single society.

The single, cross-sectional study and the longitudinal study based on the single cohort can be considered restricted cases of period analysis and cohort analysis, respectively. Cross-sectional studies compare people at different points in the life cycle, thereby confusing the effects of aging with unique cohort characteristics. Panel studies trace the same individuals from one time to the next, tracking the social, psychological, and biological consequences of aging. However, they risk confounding aging and period effects. Moreover, as Riley emphasizes,

> In a cross sectional study, restricted to a single period there is no possibility of generalizing across periods, studying period differences, or assessing period effects. And in a longitudinal study, restricted to a single cohort, there is no possibility of generalizing across co-

TABLE 5.2

Table 5.1 Adapted for Period Analysis

Age (years)	Years of Observation				
	1939	1949	1959	1969	1976
8–17	1922–31 (Cohort A)	1932–41 (Cohort H)	1942–51 (Cohort I)	1952–61 (Cohort J)	1959–68
18–27	1912–21 (Cohort B)	1922–31	1932–41	1942–51	1949–58
28–37	1902–11 (Cohort C)	1912–21	1922–31	1932–41	1939–48
38–47	1892–01 (Cohort D)	1902–11	1912–21	1922–31	1929–38
48–57	1882–91 (Cohort E)	1892–01	1902–11	1912–21	1919–28
58–67	1872–81 (Cohort F)	1882–91	1892–01	1902–11	1909–18
68–77	1862–71	1872–81	1882–91	1892–01	1899–08

Source: Compiled by the author.

horts, studying cohort differences, or assessing cohort
effects. [1972, p. 77]

Yet, cohort analysis is plagued with its own set of problems,
which are best reviewed now. First, in examining a cohort table
there are logical questions of what assumptions to make in attributing
particular findings to aging effects, to cohort effects, or to period
effects. Conflicts in interpretation are possible because both age and
cohort effects can explain the cross-sectional data in each column;
age and period effects are confounded in each cohort diagonal, and cohort and period effects in each row. This is an example of what Blalock (1960, 1966) has called

the identification problem, which occurs when an independent variable in an analysis is a perfect function of
two (or more) other variables of theoretical interest.
[1966, p. 52]

(See Glenn 1977; Riley, Johnson, and Foner 1972; Ryder 1964; Schaie
1965.) Riley, Johnson, and Foner and Glenn both emphasize that si-
multaneous use of data for different age levels, cohorts, and periods
can provide tentative evidence in identifying which theoretical factors
explain the empirical regularities (Glenn 1977, p. 14). Since a statistical solution to the logical problem of the confounding of the three effects does not exist, theory and evidence from outside the table itself
and, as Glen states, "Any knowledge one has, from any source" (1977,
p. 16) should be used to interpret the separate effects of aging, period,
and cohort effects. In this analysis, changes in female data are con-
trasted with changes in male data to facilitate the interpretation of
sex-specific and sex-role-related patterns.
    Second, because the size and composition of a cohort may change
through the death and migration of individuals, it is possible to attribute changes in the composition of the cohort to changes in the propensities or capacities of individuals. Or, the compositional change may
reduce the variation by offsetting other influences. If the theoretical
interest is with the effect of aging on individuals, changes in the composition of the cohort may lead to interpretative confusion. In criminological studies such as this one, the well-known effects of migration and mortality as well as incarceration alter the composition
of the cohort. It has been noted that older citizens commit less serious offenses (Riley and Foner 1968; Sutherland and Cressey 1978).
This finding may be due in part to the mortality or incarceration of
the most violent recidivists. For example, in this study the re-
searcher was aware that several juveniles with long criminal records
were killed in the 1960s and therefore could not figure in the data for

1976. Fortunately, the population of Metroville and its economic position in the county have remained relatively stable, as has its racial
composition, over the last 40 years.

Third, a cohort analysis uses aggragate data that records net
changes, obscuring individual shifts that may offset each other. Individuals, shifting in opposite directions, can counteract each other
in the collective data for the cohort. Although particular individuals
cannot be identified over time, a sequence of cross-sectional studies
does have the advantage of avoiding the special difficulties of longitudinal designs in attracting and holding panelists.

The advantages of cohort analysis are in exploring assumptions
about aging, its effect on allocation to roles, and the behavioral uniqueness of different cohorts. The assumption of sex role theory is that
there have been cohort or period changes in the criminal behavior of
females. Cohort differences are a product of changes in childhood
socialization that affect allocation to roles. Period effects are the
result of changes in the legitimate and illegitimate opportunity structure available to women.

In order to clarify the relationships among aging, cohort flow,
and the forces of social stability and change, separate cohort tables
for males and females with seriousness of offense as the dependent
variable have been computed. First, the intracohort pattern for males
and females born in the same period was examined for a sequence of
cohorts. What is the age at which seriousness of offense peaks? Is
this different for males and females of the same birth cohort? Are
the differences between cohorts significant? Moreover, do male and
female cohorts change over time in similar ways? Second, a period
analysis helps determine if historical conditions have precipitated a
change in seriousness of offense that was not restricted to one age
stratum. Our interest is in sex-specific period changes that may have
affected one or more age strata.

INTRACOHORT PATTERNS AND COHORT DIFFERENCES

In Tables 5.3 and 5.4 the intracohort pattern for a sequence of
cohorts is examined.

Note the life-cycle pattern of seriousness of offense of a cohort.
Numerous studies have noted that the rate of criminality is highest
among the young (especially juveniles), but the most serious offenses,
violent personal offenses, occur later in life in the mature years.
However, among older people arrests are predominantly for crimes
against public order such as drunkenness and vagrancy. The decrease
in the seriousness of offense and in the likelihood of committing an
offense (Glaser 1964; Riley and Foner 1968, p. 402) among older

TABLE 5.3

Intracohort Analysis: Mean Seriousness of Female Arrests for
Cohorts A through J, in Sample Years Indicated
(sample size)

Cohort	Rossi's Seriousness Scores for Offenses*				
	1939	1949	1959	1969	1976
J (1952–61)	—	—	—	—	—
I (1942–51)	—	—	—	—	—
H (1932–41)	—	—	—	—	—
A (1922–31)	—	3.53 (1)	4.91 (25)	4.41 (160)	—
B (1912–21)	4.35 (12)	3.53 (7)	4.49 (7)	5.49 (20)	4.72 (109)
C (1902–11)	4.96 (8)	4.18 (8)	4.58 (7)	5.11 (13)	5.14 (32)
D (1892–01)	0.00 (0)	3.53 (5)	4.77 (19)	4.49 (8)	5.68 (6)
E (1882–91)	3.53 (3)	4.07 (3)	3.53 (2)	5.23 (4)	3.53 (2)
F (1872–81)	3.53 (1)	0.00 (0)	3.53 (2)	0.00 (0)	4.06 (4)
G (1862–71)	0.00	0.00	0.00	0.00	3.53 (4)

Note: See Table 2.2.

Source: Compiled by the author.

people may be due to a number of factors. Adults may, over their
lifetime, learn to conform or learn to escape detection by committing
crimes that are either not prosecuted or not easily detected. Aging
may discourage criminal activity requiring agility or strength.

In order to facilitate the analysis of intracohort patterns, profiles comparing males and females of the same birth cohort are presented in Figures 5.1–5.6. These profiles are based on the data in
the diagonals of Tables 5.3 (females) and 5.4 (males). Profiles were
drawn by plotting the mean seriousness of offense for each cohort by
the median of the cohort during the year in which arrests were

TABLE 5.4

Intracohort Analysis: Mean Seriousness of Male Arrests for
Cohorts A through J, in Sample Years Indicated
(sample size)

Cohort	Rossi's Seriousness Scores for Offenses*				
	1939	1949	1959	1969	1976
J (1952–61)	—	—	—	—	—
I (1942–51)	—	—	—	—	—
H (1932–41)	—	—	—	—	—
A (1922–31)	—	4.78 (6)	4.79 (62)	4.54 (112)	—
B (1912–21)	3.88 (37)	4.16 (75)	4.53 (44)	5.35 (38)	5.11 (71)
C (1902–11)	4.03 (62)	4.24 (62)	4.69 (35)	5.48 (20)	5.06 (33)
D (1892–01)	3.98 (45)	3.60 (71)	4.88 (39)	4.64 (17)	5.59 (13)
E (1882–91)	3.72 (28)	3.59 (63)	3.81 (29)	5.67 (6)	3.98 (12)
F (1872–81)	4.14 (6)	3.61 (40)	3.83 (20)	3.53 (6)	5.22 (5)
G (1862–71)	—	3.53 (13)	3.53 (2)	—	—

Note: See Table 2.2.

Source: Compiled by the author.

sampled. From Table 5.1, it is clear that there are 11 cohorts defined in the data. The youngest, cohort K, was born in 1962–71 and
was between 8 and 17 years of age in 1976. The oldest, cohort G,
was born in 1862–71 and was between 68 and 77 years of age in 1939.
Obviously for these cohorts there is only data at one age and, therefore, life-cycle patterns are not presented. Profiles are not drawn
for cohorts F (1872–81), E (1882–91), or D (1892–1902) because the
life-cycle data are truncated to include only the later years, which
criminologically are less interesting and methodologically are troubled
by compositional flaws referred to earlier. However, of the six male

FIGURE 5.1

Mean Crime Seriousness by Age for Males and Females Born in the
Period 1922-31
(Cohort A)

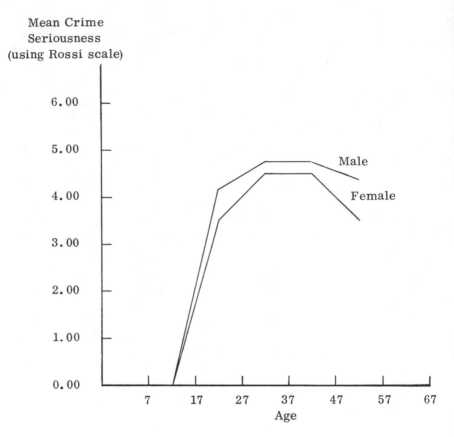

and six female cohorts graphed, several interesting points emerge,
which are supported, in addition, by the data in Tables 5.3 and 5.4
for cohorts D, E, and F.

First, it is most interesting to note that in each of the Figures
5.1 through 5.6, males and females of the same cohort reach their
peak in seriousness of offense at the same point in the life cycle. The
age of most serious criminality varies from cohort to cohort, although for most cohorts (A, B, C, D, E, and F) it occurs in the adult
years: for cohorts A (1922-31) and C (1902-11), in the 28-37 year
period; for cohorts B (1912-21) and E (1882-91), in the 48-57 year
period; for cohort H, in the 38-47 year period. Interestingly, for
the more recent cohorts (I and J), seriousness peaks in the earlier

years of the 18-27 year period. Note that for all cohorts, the age of most serious criminality is the same for males and females. Even the jump in seriousness to the earlier age groups evidenced by cohorts I and J is common to both males and females. Of course, the life-cycle data for these cohorts is not complete and any pattern seen in the cohorts at this point may not be maintained. However, cross-sectional data have emphasized the preponderance of violent crimes in the 15-19 and 20-24 age groups (U.S., Department of Justice, FBI 1975, pp. 188-89) and support these data.

Not only is the age of most serious criminality identical for males and females of the same cohort, but there is also a basic similarity between the life-cycle patterns of the two sexes in any cohort.

FIGURE 5.2

Mean Crime Seriousness by Age for Males and Females Born in the
Period 1912-21
(Cohort B)

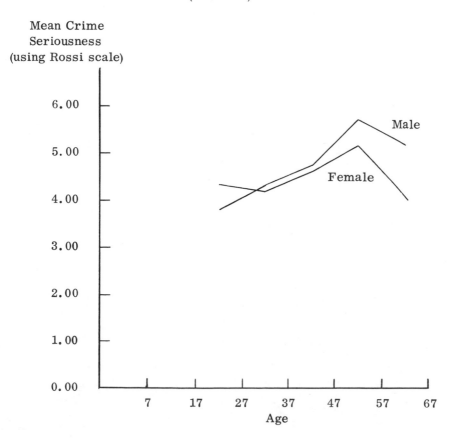

That is, there is more similarity in the life-cycle patterns of different sexes of the same generation than there is between the life-cycle
phases for different cohorts of the same sex. Figures 5.7 (females)
and 5.8 (males) illustrate the uniqueness of each age in the life cycle
for different cohorts. Although, generally, older people (as indicated
by the literature) are least criminalistic, there are few other com-
monalities among the same-sex cohorts. For example, each cohort
peaks at a different age, and the range of criminality is small for
some cohorts and much larger for others. Since data for several cohorts are not complete for the entire life cycle, these findings are
merely suggestive. Nevertheless, these data imply that cohorts appear to be responding to forces other than chronological age. Differ-

FIGURE 5.3

Mean Crime Seriousness by Age for Males and Females Born in the
Period 1902-11
(Cohort C)

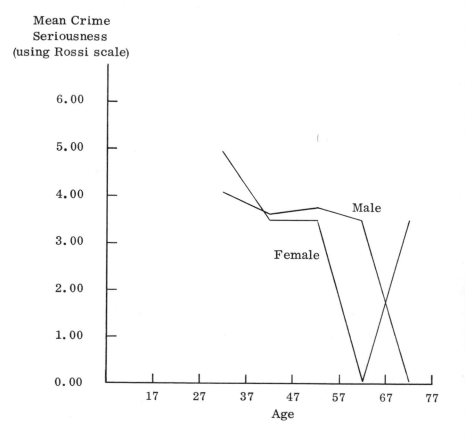

FIGURE 5.4

Mean Crime Seriousness by Age for Males and Females Born in the
Period 1932-41
(Cohort H)

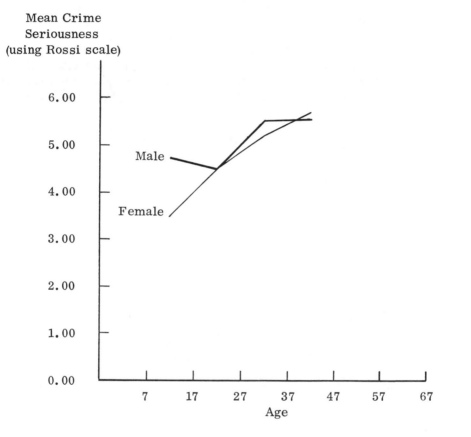

ent cohorts of the same-sex evidence more variation than same-age
cohorts of different sexes.

Interestingly, there is nothing in the criminological literature
that would have predicted these findings. Normally, the differences
between male and female criminality are emphasized. The traditional cross-sectional study emphasizes the varied and violent nature of male crime, frequently ignoring the pattern and incidence of
female crime. Since cohort data are difficult and frequently impossible to compile, cohort analyses of criminological patterns are
rare. These cohort differences suggest the significance of social
trends in influencing socialization patterns, regardless of sex. These
cohort patterns, by their consistency, emphasize the uniqueness of

the historical period in which the individual lives. Amazingly, co-horts are truly different. Whether one is male or female is relatively insignificant in comparison to the impact of the social currents of the time in which one lives.

PERIOD ANALYSIS

With Table 5.5 (females) and Table 5.6 (males) age-specific period comparison can be made for each sex. Using the information in these two tables, it is possible to compare change over time in the seriousness of female arrests with change in male arrest seriousness

FIGURE 5.5

Mean Crime Seriousness by Age for Males and Females Born in the
Period 1942–51
(Cohort I)

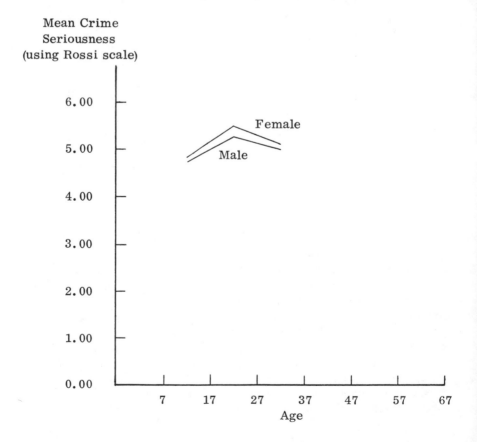

FIGURE 5.6

Mean Crime Seriousness by Age for Males and Females Born in the
Period 1952-61
(Cohort J)

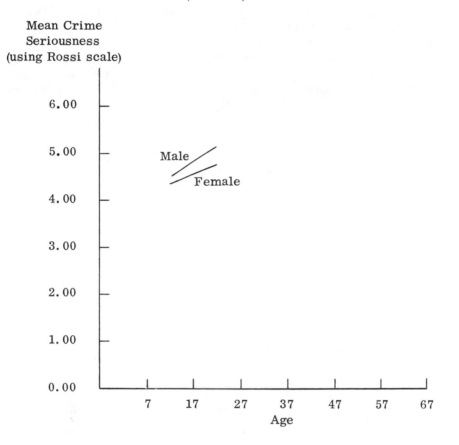

for the same period. Our interest here is in the degree to which period changes have been similar for males and females of the same
age. In Table 5.7 the information from Tables 5.5 and 5.6 is dis-
tilled for the analysis below.

For the period 1959-69 there is no significant difference between the change for males and the change for females. For every
age group, the direction of change for males and females is the same,
and the extent of change is not significantly different. Thus, it appears that any change among females between 1959 and 1969 in seriousness of arrests was not sex-role-related. On the other hand,
it is of course possible that males and females each responded to

different (and possibly sex-role-related) period effects that resulted in a similar increase by age in seriousness of arrests.

Looking again at Table 5.7, we note that from 1949 to 1959 the change among males was similar in direction and extent to the change among females, except for the youngest age group. Among the 8-17 year olds, the males decreased slightly in seriousness of arrests (-.20) while the females increased measurably (+1.33). Interestingly, this cohort had the highest mean seriousness of arrests (4.86) in 1959, as juveniles, and again in 1969 as young adults (5.44). While not the highest in 1976, this cohort continues to include the more serious female offenders. Thus, the age group that is the most aggres-

FIGURE 5.7

Mean Crime Seriousness by Age for Females Born in Different
Periods
(cohorts are indicated by letter)

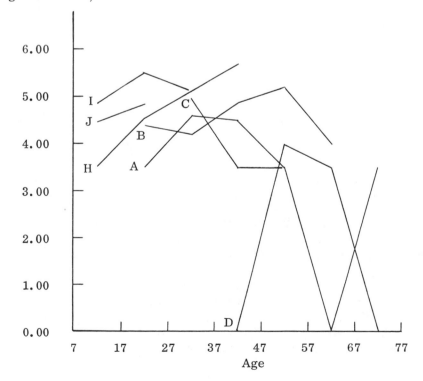

FIGURE 5. 8

Mean Crime Seriousness by Age for Males Born in Different Periods
(cohorts are indicated by letter)

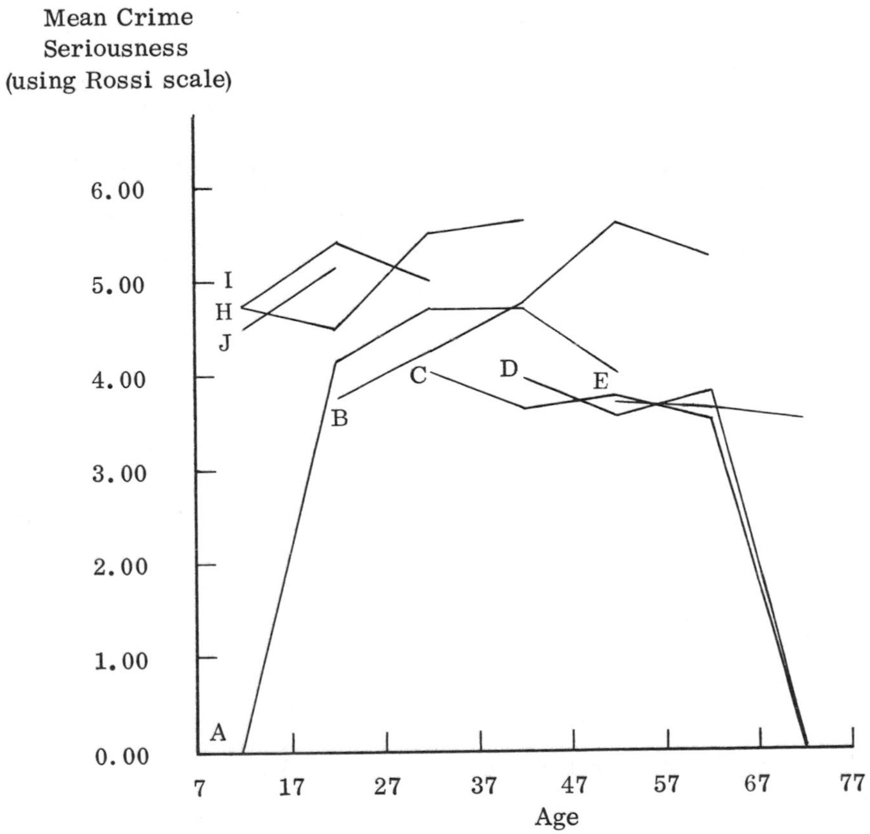

Mean Crime
Seriousness
(using Rossi scale)

sive in 1969, the 18-27 year olds, is also the cohort that was most
aggressive in 1959. Thus, an analysis of period effects suggests
that, whereas increasing seriousness of arrests among 18-27 year
old females in 1969 might have been interpreted as the result of sex-
role-related desires for increased opportunity for success, it is perhaps more credible to interpret this phenomenon as a cohort effect
not related to sex-specific social movements but to historical or
demographic characteristics of the cohort. This cohort (born 1942-
51) has evidenced a consistent pattern over time. It is the cohort
that initiated the trend to increasing seriousness of criminal activity
at an earlier age. And over its (limited) life cycle, it continues to
be more likely than other cohorts to act aggressively. If the pattern

TABLE 5.5

Period Analysis: Mean Seriousness of Female Arrests by Age for
Cohorts A through J
(sample size)

Age[a] (years)	Rossi's Seriousness Scores for Offenses[b]				
	1939	1949	1959	1969	1976
8–17	—	3.53 (1)	4.86 (26)	4.41 (160)	4.46 (115)
18–27	4.35 (12)	3.53 (7)	4.65 (6)	5.44 (23)	5.48 (47)
28–37	4.96 (8)	4.18 (8)	4.58 (7)	5.12 (10)	5.20 (23)
38–47	—	3.53 (5)	4.77 (19)	4.56 (9)	6.06 (2)
48–57	3.53 (3)	—	3.53 (2)	5.26 (3)	3.53 (2)
58–67	3.53 (1)	—	3.53 (2)	3.53 (2)	3.79 (8)
68–77	—	—	—	4.07 (3)	—

[a]Table 5.2 is the key to cohorts in period analysis.
[b]See Table 2.2.

Source: Compiled by the author.

that is suggested by the data is valid, it is difficult to know precisely why this is so. Interestingly, this cohort, born 1942–51, is the one that is usually described as the "baby boom" cohort. It is possible that its increased size resulted in increased competitiveness for the legitimate and illegitimate slots available.

Returning to Table 5.7, we note that the period 1969–76 has resulted in somewhat greater activity among male cohorts than among female cohorts. The three youngest female age groups—8–17, 18–27, and 28–37—have shown the least amount of change. While there has been a very slight increase in seriousness of arrests among females, the direction of change among male cohorts has been more mixed. Those two female age groups in which there has been much change—38-47 and 48-57—include the smallest number of offenders and, therefore, it is likely that variation is due to sampling error. A t-test finds no statistically significant difference between any female age group from 1969 to 1976. Thus, change among female cohorts in seriousness of arrests has dropped off by 1976. Among males more change is evident. There is a statistically significant difference between juveniles (8-17) in 1969 and 1976 and between 28-37 year olds in 1969 and 1976. Statistically significant change is al-

TABLE 5.6

Period Analysis: Mean Seriousness of Male Arrests by Age for Cohorts A through J
(sample size)

Age[a] (years)	Rossi's Seriousness Scores for Offenses[b]				
	1939	1949	1959	1969	1976
8-17	—	4.98 (7)	4.78 (65)	4.55 (113)	5.23 (91)
18-27	3.88 (37)	4.13 (74)	4.53 (41)	5.37 (38)	5.17 (41)
28-37	4.03 (62)	4.24 (62)	4.69 (35)	5.45 (20)	4.90 (20)
38-47	3.98 (45)	3.60 (71)	4.88 (39)	4.61 (17)	5.57 (10)
48-57	3.72 (28)	3.59 (63)	3.81 (29)	5.67 (6)	4.30 (11)
58-67	4.14 (6)	3.61 (40)	3.83 (20)	3.53 (6)	4.07 (3)
68-77	3.53 (5)	3.53 (13)	3.53 (2)	—	—

[a]Table 5.2 is the key to cohorts in period analysis.
[b]See Table 2.2.

Source: Compiled by the author.

TABLE 5.7

Change in Mean Seriousness of Arrests in Selected Periods by Sex and Age

Age* (years)	1949–59		1959–69		1969–76	
	Male	Female	Male	Female	Male	Female
8–17	−0.20	+1.33	−0.23	−0.45	+0.68	+0.05
18–27	+0.40	+1.12	+0.84	+0.79	−0.20	+0.04
28–37	+0.45	+0.40	+0.76	+0.54	−0.55	+0.08
38–47	+1.24	+1.24	−0.27	−0.21	+0.96	+1.50
48–57	+0.22	—	+1.86	+1.73	−1.37	−1.73
58–67	+0.22	—	−0.30	—	+0.54	+0.26
68–77	—	—	—	—	—	—

*Table 5.2 is keyed to cohorts.

Note: Change is measured in number of points on Rossi's Seriousness Scores for Offenses, Tables 5.5 and 5.6.

Source: Compiled by the author.

most reached among the older age groups—38-47 and 48-57. Thus, the 1969-76 period has been more volatile for males than females.

CONCLUSION

In conclusion, while age effects have always been real factors influencing the life-cycle pattern of criminal activity, the data suggest unique cohort differences that are consistent for males and females. In addition, cohort effects seem more powerful than period effects in defining change in seriousness of criminal activity. And cohort differences are more probably related to historical and demographic characteristics than sex-role-related social movements.

6

CONCLUSION

This chapter is a summary of the findings and the alternative hypotheses that explicate them. The research began with two alternative hypotheses to explain the rise in the female arrest rate: (1) the impact of the women's movement and (2) the effect of change in the likelihood of arrest as a result of organizational pressures within the police department. A summary of the empirical evidence probing each hypothesis and a review of the serendipitous findings on the significance of cohort (as opposed to period) differences are presented.

REVIEW OF THE EVIDENCE ON THE IMPACT OF THE WOMEN'S MOVEMENT ON ARREST RATES

This research has shown that arrests in 1969 were unique in several respects—most notably in quantity and type of offender. The number of female arrests increased markedly, as did the percentage of white, higher-class, juvenile, female offenders—many of whom were first offenders. Juvenile friendship networks in 1969 indicated a greater propensity for girls to commit offenses in groups and to be arrested for more serious offenses than previously or than mixed groups were. The kinds of offenses most frequently committed in Metroville—drugs and fraud and forgery—were typical of the pattern nationwide.

Interestingly, those aspects of the arrest pattern that were distinctive in 1969 were not repeated in 1976. Whereas the women's movement was just gaining momentum in 1969, it had become a more accepted and established movement in 1976, having achieved gains in modifying social arrangements (Freeman 1975; Hole and Levine 1971). If sex role changes were the effective causal agents, one would assume the character of arrests in 1976 to be similar to that in 1969. However, even in the juvenile data where the trends most consistent with presumed sex role change were found, there was indication that 1976 arrests did not follow the pattern established in 1969. Female juveniles were less likely in 1976 to act in groups, and while mixed-sex groups were more deviant in 1976, the role females play in this deviance was unknown.

The focus on 1969 as a way of proving that anatomy is not destiny (which certainly is partly the motivation of Adler [1975], Simon [1975], Hoffman-Bustamante [1973], and others) should not obscure the larger, more interesting story in this longitudinal data on female criminality. While there was a marked increase in arrests between 1959 and 1969, there was a significant increase between 1949 and 1959 also. In fact, both periods were quite similar in many respects: (1) the female arrest rate rose faster than that of males; (2) changes in criminal activity were greater among juveniles than among adults; (3) white females experienced higher arrest-rate increases than black females; (4) a greater percentage of whites than blacks were arrested for drugs, fraud and forgery, and the less serious property offenses; (5) a greater percentage of blacks than whites were arrested for assault, serious property offenses, and the more serious crimes against people; and (6) first offenders were most likely to be juveniles (modal age was 15-17 years). Thus, it is difficult to credit the woman's movement with these changes, since much of what is considered, criminologically, a product of the women's movement was evident in the previous decade, 1949-59.

The hypothesized connection between arrest increases and the women's movement is further weakened when arrests in 1976 are compared with those in 1969—both periods of sex role change; 1976 was different from 1969 in several respects. Contrary to the case in 1969, in 1976 we found that (1) more blacks than whites (female) were arrested; (2) more lower-class females were arrested than higher-class females; (3) a greater percentage of black females than white females were arrested for drugs, fraud and forgery, and personal offenses; and (4) female juveniles were less likely to be arrested in groups.

Thus, I contend that the women's movement did not have a long-range or lasting impact on arrest rates. Since the correlation between the sex ratio in arrests and the role of women in society is well accepted (Sutherland 1978), it is important to try to understand why a movement that presumably affected social and cultural arrangements between the sexes did not have a more profound impact on crime rates.

Whereas Adler (1975) stressed the impact of the rhetoric of the movement in altering self-image and Simon (1975) emphasized the role of increased opportunities, it was Hoffman-Bustamante (1973)

who suggested how sex role theory might be wedded to traditional criminological paradigms so that both the observed sex ratio in arrests
and the lack of more significant change are explained.

TOWARD A REVISION OF TRADITIONAL CRIMINOLOGICAL THEORY

In the literature a line has been drawn between male and female
criminality, marking the two as inescapably different from each other.
For example, studying women incarcerated for crimes of violence,
Ward (1969) found that "most of the theories of crime causation are
inappropriate when applied to female offenders" (p. 907). Harris be-
moans the critical weakness of contemporary criminal deviance theories whose explanatory power he claims "is only marginally greater
than it was in the phrenologists' day" (1977, p. 3). This defect results from

> the continuing failure to consider women, and conse-
> quently, the sex variable in such theory. . . . General
> theories of criminal deviance are now no more than spe-
> cial theories of male deviance. [1977, p. 4]

He corrects this conceptual blindness through the development of "a
functional theory of deviant type-scripts" (p. 3). It can also be cor-
rected by wedding sex role theory to traditional criminological thinking so that the cultural imperatives that prescribe sex role ideology
explain the differential impact on the sexes of the critical variables
employed in traditional criminological theories.

Taking Harris's (1977) advice that theories should "not merely
'take account' of the sex variable, but rather instead start with it"
(p. 4), this research begins by noting that there are indeed sex roles
in this culture that define the appropriate attitudes, behavior, and
ambitions of each sex. These roles are not only sex specific but class
specific. That is, the sex role of the lower-class male is not necessarily the same as that of the middle-class male, as the sex role of
the lower-class female is not the same as that of the middle-class
female. The extent of role differentiation affects criminality by
shaping the definition of appropriate goals, suitable means to those
goals, and "self attributions" (Harris, 1977). Wise (1967) notes that
in the middle class "female delinquency closely resembles male delinquency in form and quantity" (p. 183) because the male and female
role definitions and expectations in the family, school, and peer
group are more similar for middle-class boys and girls than they
are for their lower-class counterparts. The trivial and nonviolent

character of middle-class delinquency is attributed to "the more per-
vasive feminization of middle class boys as compared to working class
boys" (Weis 1976, p. 5). There is a convergence of male and female
sex roles in the middle class that is not found in the lower class or
working class (Bahr, Bowerman, and Gecas 1974; Kamarovsky 1962;
Lopata 1971).

Hoffman-Bustamante's contribution was to emphasize the importance of sex role socialization in determining the probability of
criminal behavior. Her delineation of differential role expectations
for men and women, sex differences in socialization practices, structurally determined differences in opportunities to commit particular
offenses, and differential access or pressures toward criminally
oriented subcultures and careers is a clear explication of sex role
ideology, but it ignores the key elements in criminal deviance theories that must be redefined in sex role terms so that the traditional
theories have broader explanatory power.

To examine the theories, Harris's (1977) set of conceptual elements—goal utility, behavior utility, probability, and self-attribution—
were adopted, and his lead was followed in considering how structured
strain, differential opportunity, differential association, control theory, and self-attribution theories can generalize to more than the
male population. Harris accepts as a given a social structure which
distributes opportunities and rewards differentially along ethnic, class,
and race lines. To this given add the notion of sex roles differentiated
by sex and class (and perhaps race). If an understanding of sex roles
is included as part of the cultural backdrop, traditional theories do
explain the sex ratios in criminality, and, importantly, an explanation of why the women's movement failed to impact on the crime rate
in a lasting way is possible.

Structured Strain

Harris reduces Merton's (1938) theory to the propositional statements that (1) when the probability of goal utility through criminal
means is greater than the probability of goal utility through legitimate
means (P GU/L) (and assuming that the probability of goal utility
through legitimate means is distributed by the social structure) and
(2) behavioral utility through legitimate means is low, then (3) the
probability of criminal behavior is greater than the probability of legitimate behavior. Harris (1977) maintains that in order to consider
the sex variable,

> strain theory would seem to require that its major ele-
> ment, P GU/L, be distributed by sex . . . however, the

theory becomes counterfactual: since women appear to
have lesser access to goal utility via the array of legitimate opportunities available than men do, women
should show a higher crime rate (if only for economi-
cally-related crimes) than men. Clearly, they do not.
[1977, p. 7]

However, the logical structure of strain theory is maintained and its
conclusions sustained if the definition of goals for men and women is
informed by sex role theory. For the lower-class male, the goal is
"making it"—money, social status, and if possible, power, to be
achieved ideally through legitimate endeavor; if necessary, and if opportunity avails, through illegitimate means. For the middle-class
female the goals are the same but the legitimate means are expanded
to include marriage. On the street (and in the sociologists' theories)
a women's social position is measured (literally and figuratively) by
first her father's accomplishments and then her husband's. Means
to a favored social class position for a female are in the use of her
personal attributes to gain a husband of position or potential. Certainly the legitimate means to this goal utility (cultivating esteemed
personal qualities and being in a place where suitable candidates
abound) are greater than the probability of goal utility through criminal
means (prostitution, blackmail, grand larceny). Lower-class boys
have higher crime rates than middle-class girls because the probability of them achieving their material goals through legitimate means
is much less secure than that of middle-class girls. Her goals are
much more likely to be achieved by legitimate than criminal means.
Interestingly, the crimes of most middle-class girls are the goal
utility acts of shoplifting cosmetics and clothing or fraud and forgery,
which is shoplifting with the use of a false credit card. It has been
widely accepted that lower-class, black females are more likely to
commit crimes than middle-class females. This is consistent with
the fact that "good marriages," that is, marriages that assure financial solvency and security, are less available to them and individual
effort in "making it" is more of a necessity.

Differential Opportunity

To structured-strain theory is added the notion that the probability of criminal behavior is greater than the probability of legitimate behavior when both the probability of goal utility through criminal means and the probability of goal utility through legitimate means
are differentially distributed by social-structural factors, such as
class, caste, ethnicity, and area. Harris objects that this does not
explain why the sex ratio for violent crimes is higher than the sex

ratio for property crimes, since violent criminal means are more equally distributed than property-oriented criminal means "because of women's traditional location in the home" (1977, p. 7). On the contrary, Hoffman-Bustamante explains very well the socialization of women that leads to a self-image (what Harris might conceptualize as a "self-attribution") of vulnerability and weakness. Girls who are raised to be nurturant, maternal, warm, and sympathetic have a difficult time being violent toward those they believe to be stronger than themselves. For these reasons, women's violent crimes are committed against children, incapacitated (through sleep or alcohol) men, or with the help of strong able-bodied males (Ward 1969). Ward has noted

> that the participation of women in robbery and burglary was not consistent with the criminal role males play in these crimes but that their behavior was consistent with their role as women. [1969, p. 906]

On the other hand, despite the objective physical limitations a lower-class boy may have, his self-concept (as decreed by peer-enforced sex roles) demands toughness, strength, and the use of physical force to prove his "manhood" and protect his "rep," as countless junkies-turned-sociologists have described for us in autobiographical accounts (Brown 1965; Rettig, Torres, and Garrett 1977; Thomas 1967). This is especially intriguing since the "macho" ethic is strongest in the Hispanic culture, where physical size is slight but the necessity to prove one's physical prowess is overpowering. A sense of vulnerability or strength is determined for men and women not, in large part, by physical size, but rather by self-image, which is a function of sex roles.

Harris's second objection to differential-opportunity theory relates to the fact that if this approach were correct the marked decrease in the sex ratio for property-crime arrests in general and for white-collar, economic crimes in particular that has been found in the past few decades would apply to those over 18 and in the labor force and not, as has been observed, for those under 18. Even this can be explained by sex roles. Sex roles are, for the individual, most fluid in youth. By adulthood the individual has a firm notion of his own "feminity" or "masculinity" and to abrogate it is difficult. In contrast, the juvenile is more likely to experiment with sex-role-inappropriate behavior to learn the consequences of violating the norms.

Differential Association

Although Harris dismisses Sutherland's (1939) theory as being too imprecise and "unspecified" to be scrutinized by introducing the sex variable, it is clear that social controls in the family restrict the "associations" of girls more than boys (compare Nye [1958] and Toby [1957]), and that legal social controls (use of police and truant officers) are utilized more readily in the protection of girls than boys. Informal interviews with a current juvenile officer attested to the higher number of parental referrals for female incorrigibility, runaways, and truancy than for males. Certainly the "associations" and time spent away from the parental residence of a middle-class female are more strictly monitored than that of a lower-class male.

Subcultural Differences

In this perspective,

low perceived access to legitimate goal utility leads classes of structurally disadvantaged actors to generate higher levels of behavior utility for criminal choice and lower levels of behavior utility for legitimate choice. [Harris 1977, p. 8]

But, as Harris (1977) argues, this suggests that since women are more blocked from goal utility via legitimate means than men, they would develop, relative to men, higher levels of criminal behavior utility and, consequently, higher levels of crime. This interpretation is based on a faulty definition of female goals and access to those goals, as was stated in the section on structured strain. Moreover, women are taught to compete with other women for the affection and attention of men. Women are not socialized to look to other women for help in achieving their societal goals—other women are their natural competitors.

Control

Hirschi's (1969) control theory postulates that commitment to conventional activities and conventional others is the major social determinant of commitment to legitimate behavior utility. It is this commitment to conventional activities and others that outweighs the goal utility to be gained through criminal behavior and, literally, "controls" criminal behavior. Harris is not convinced that, for juveniles and adults alike, females are more committed to conventional activities than males, though he notes that the theory is "not contraindicated by much existing theory or research" (p. 9). Certainly for female, middle-class adults, the conventional family-home-children model is very compelling. Without it, one is invisible in the social world. With it, a successful life can be extracted from voluntary activities and the vicarious enjoyment of the accomplishments of one's family. These goals are much more readily achievable through legitimate behavior than criminal behavior.

For the lower-class male, this middle-class image of adult life is irrelevant to his goals of "making it." In fact, material success and position may be more readily achieved through criminal behavior than through legitimate behavior. As middle-class men and women are more likely to accept this conventional orientation to adult life, so are they less likely to evidence criminal behavior than lower-class men or women, for whom the pay-offs from this model may not be as real.

Self-Attribution

Containment theory and labeling theory are classified by Harris's (1977) concept of self-attribution. That is,

> the actor perceives himself or herself as "the type of person expected to do L or C's. . . . Self-attribution which produces deviance has the propositional form, 'since I am a member of the class of people X, then, I expect myself to produce more of behavior Y than non members of X.'" [1977, p. 110]

Certainly sex role ideology explains one's "self-attributions." Whether one considers oneself nurturant or tough, vulnerable or strong, protected or protector is determined by one's self-image as man or woman. Harris implies as much when he declares "self-attributions are very clearly tied to and distributed by sex in this, if not in all societies" (1977, p. 10).

As containment theory finds pressure toward deviance distributed by neighborhood or area, so too are sex roles distinct in Hispanic communities, middle-class communities, white communities, black communities, rural communities, urban communities, and suburban communities. The alleged sex role differences between men and women and the relative importance of those differences varies by neighborhood and area and affects the extent of behavioral similarity in men and women. It is this variability that results in a greater difference between the delinquency of lower-class and middle-class males than between male and female middle-class delinquency.

Similarly, consistent with labeling theory, women are more likely to be protected from the labeling power of social-control agents

because of their assumed malleability and receptivity to guidance.
Women are rarely considered intractable or, in a word, tough.

In conclusion, I contend that the traditional deviance paradigms,
informed by sex role theory, do explain the sex ratios in criminality.
From this thesis, it would seem logical to deduce that an alteration
in sex roles would, indeed, lead to an alteration in criminal sex ratios. This would be so if indeed there were a change in the key elements of sex roles that affect criminal propensity. The women's
movement has attempted a number of legislative and constitutional re-
forms, but women still know that financial security may be gained
through marriage, as well as by individual effort; that while it is permissible to be assertive, it is still not permissible to be aggressive
or violent; that other women are their competitors for male affection
and now for competence; and that women are not "the type" to commit
criminal behavior (self-attributions). That is, the revolution in sex
roles has been a quiet, legislative one. Many things have not changed:
female self-attributions and associational networks. The definition
of acceptable female goals has simply been expanded to include competence in the work world.

Traditional criminological paradigms explain how a social movement may affect crime rates. Different theories emphasize different
intervening variables. Strain theory and differential-opportunity theory
emphasize the importance of a change in culturally defined goals for
women concomitant with a lack of legitimate means to these goals and
access to illegitimate means. Differential-association and subcultural-
difference theories stress the importance of associational or friendship networks in providing the techniques (skills), rationalizations,
and attitudes conducive to the use of delinquent behavior. Control theory emphasizes changes in the family social-control system that allows deviant behavior. Containment theory emphasizes a change in
the self-attributions that permit formally proscribed activities. Therefore, if the women's movement were to affect crime rates, it would
be through affecting self-attributions, associational networks, the
family's social control, or definitions of cultural goals and concomitant access to illegal opportunities.

Consistent with this thinking, it is possible to view the rise in
arrests in 1969 as a function of a change in associational networks
among juveniles. As friendship networks changed, an increase in
seriousness of offense activity was observed. A reversal to traditional associational patterns was correlated with reduced offense seriousness in 1976. This analysis is supported by Giordano's findings
that the female peer group can exert a strong delinquent influence.
She reports,

> it was found that the most group support for engaging in
> delinquent activities came from other girlfriends and

that perception of approval from girlfriends was significantly correlated with actual delinquent involvement.
[1976, p. 21]

This change in associational patterns may have been brought on
by the widespread publicity given to the rhetoric of the movement in
1969. Giordano has found "a significant correlation between liberality
of sex role attitudes and extent of delinquent involvement for the whites
in the sample" (1976, p. 25). Her study is the only one that suggests
the way in which adherence to a "liberated" ideology may be linked
with delinquent behavior. These data support her findings in also
showing a correlation between associational patterns and delinquent
activity. These data are predicted by subcultural-difference and differential-association theories.

It is important to note that in 1976 there was a return to the
original, traditional friendship patterns and offense activity of female
juveniles. This suggests that as the rhetoric of the movement was
given less publicity, juveniles were less influenced by it.

ALTERNATIVE HYPOTHESES

Review of Evidence on the Impact of Police
Activity on Crime Rates

It is also necessary to evaluate the validity of the police-activity
hypothesis and the findings of the cohort analysis in explaining the
quantity and quality of offense behavior over time.

It was noted in Chapter 1 that an increase in arrests may be
due not to a change in the behavior of women, but rather to a change
in the behavior of the police. Specifically, increases may be the result of a change in the likelihood of arrest due to an increase in the
willingness of the police to view female behavior as culpable.

In support of this hypothesis, there is the sudden and sharp rise
in male and female juvenile arrests upon the appointment of a new
juvenile officer in 1968. However, an examination of the type of arrests that increased did not show conclusively that the increase in female arrests was of a proactive (police-initiated), rather than a re-
active (citizen-initiated), nature. Moreover, the data on juvenile
friendship networks show a significant change in the pattern of female
offense activity that cannot easily be attributed to police behavior.
This in itself forces us to question the validity of the charge that the
rise in juvenile arrests is due solely to police organizational factors.

The Generational Hypothesis

From the cohort analysis it appears that offense seriousness is more highly related to cohort differences than period effects. Whereas increased seriousness of arrests among 18- to 27-year-old females in 1969 might have been interpreted as the result of sex-role-motivated actions, it appears more credible to interpret this phenomenon as a cohort effect, not related to a social movement but to historical and demographic characteristics of the cohort. This generation not only initiated the trend to increased seriousness of offense activity at an earlier age but, over its life cycle, continued to act more violently than other cohorts examined in the same cross-sectional slice. It appears that period differences (as in the extensiveness of the formal social-control system) may be less significant in influencing criminality than socialization practices and temporal conditions, which vary by cohort. This cohort, born (1942-51), was unique historically for several reasons. As the "baby boom" cohort, its numbers have always been emphasized. What is less emphasized but also true is that there may have been a breakdown in the family social-control system signaled by a divorce rate in 1945 that was not exceeded until 1974 (Faris 1974). The end of the war was a period of upheaval and change that impacted on the family structure: the return of the father, the relinquishing of wartime employment by the mother, and marital discord culminating in divorce for many. Disorganization within the family has been noted by Nye (1958), Toby (1957), and Hirschi (1969) as increasing the probability of delinquency. In addition, changes in the material conditions of consumption—increasing reliance on self-service marketing and credit purchasing—may have led to increases in certain categories of property offense.

The data are provocative. Further research should explore more precisely the significance of and forces behind cohort differences. C. Wright Mills (1967) emphasized the importance of understanding one's place in history in interpreting social facts. These findings illustrate that dictum.

APPENDIX

MULTIPLE REGRESSION RESULTS

In Tables A.1 and A.2, we examine multiple regression results. While it was not the intention of this research to determine which variables predict seriousness of offense, it is interesting, first, to note the extent of variance in seriousness of offense explained by the variables that are usually considered by sociologists quite significant—that is, sex, race, social class, and age—and, second, to examine the comparative power of the different variables to explain variance in the dependent variable.

The independent variables used in the regression equations are age, race, sex, social class, and social period. Nominal variables, such as race, sex, and social period were entered as dummy variables. The dependent variables are seriousness of first offense (Table A.1) and seriousness of offense in the sampled year (Table A.2).

TABLE A.1

Standardized Regression Coefficients for Seriousness of First Offense Regressed on All the Independent Variables Simultaneously (Model 1) and Four Selected Independent Variables (Model 2)

Independent Variables	Seriousness of First Offense	
	Model 1	Model 2
Race	-.157	-.167
Age	-.082	-.103
Sex	-.098	-.083
Year 1959	-.092	—
Year 1969	-.050	—
Social class	-.037	-.050
R^2	.056	.050

Note: All standardized regression coefficients significant at least at $p = .05$ level.

TABLE A.2

Standardized Regression Coefficients for Seriousness of Offense in
Sampled Years Regressed on All the Independent Variables
Simultaneously (Model 1) and Four Selected Independent Variables
(Model 2)

| Independent | Seriousness of Offense | |
Variables	Model 1	Model 2
Race	-.183	-.192
Age	-.060	-.077
Sex	-.077	-.064
Year 1959	-.078	—
Year 1969	-.044	—
Social class	-.035	-.046
R^2	.057	.053

Note: All standardized regression coefficients significant at the
.05 level.

In Table A.1, note that race, age, sex, social class, and social
period jointly explain only 6 percent of the variance in the dependent
variable, seriousness of first offense. Standardized regression coefficients indicate that race explains the most variance. Sex is a
better predictor of seriousness of first offense than all other variables,
other than race. Even so, it explains only a very small amount of
variance.

If the regression equation includes only the four variables
race, age, sex, and social class (Model 2), the explanatory power
of the sex variable is decreased. Race and now age explain the most
variance. Perhaps because of the interaction between age and social
period (Year 1959) (r = .36), the explanatory power of age is increased
when social period is dropped from the equation.

In Table A.2 seriousness of offense in the year sampled is regressed on the independent variables. Only 6 percent of the variance
in seriousness of offense is explained by all the variables. Again,
race is more powerful than the other variables. In this model, sex
is less powerful than race or social period (Year 1959). If social
period is dropped from the equation, race and age are still more
powerful than sex in explaining variance in the dependent variable.

Perhaps the most surprising finding here is the small amount
of variance explained by social class. This could be due to a number

of factors: the modest interaction between race and social class
($r = .35$), the inaccuracy of the measure of social class (income), or, more probably, the fact that social class is not a powerful predictor of criminality in a small urban area. Clark and Wenninger (1962) have noted that differences in criminality by area were more significant than social class differences in criminality within an area. The data are consistent with this finding, as are the conclusions of many ecological studies (Chilton 1964; Chilton and Dussich 1974; Lander 1954; Shaw and McKay 1942).

    In conclusion, the most striking findings are the amount of unexplained variance in the seriousness of offense (94 percent of the total) and the lack of power of the sex variable to predict offense seriousness.

REFERENCES

Adler, F. 1978. "A Criminologist's View of Women Terrorists."
New York Times, January 9, p. 24.

_____. 1975. Sisters in Crime. New York: McGraw-Hill.

Akman, D., A. Normandeau, and S. Turner. 1967. "The Measurement of Delinquency in Canada." Journal of Criminal Law,
Criminology and Police Science 58 (September): 330-37.

"The American Woman." 1970. Society 63 (November-December):
3-30.

Arnold, W. R. 1971. "Race and Ethnicity Relative to Other Factors
in Juvenile Court Dispositions." American Journal of Sociology
77 (September): 211-27.

Bahr, S., C. Bowerman, and V. Gecas. 1974. "Adolescent Perception of Conjugal Power." Social Forces 52 (March): 357-67.

Barker, G., and W. Adams. 1962. "Comparisons of the Delinquen-
cies of Boys and Girls." Journal of Criminal Law, Criminology
and Police Science 53: 470-75.

Biderman, A., and A. J. Reiss. 1967. "On Exploring the Dark
Figure of Crime." Annals of the American Academy of Political and Social Science 374 (November): 1-15.

Blalock, H. 1966. "The Identification Problem and Theory Building:
The Case of Status Inconsistency." American Sociological Review 31 (February): 52-61.

_____. 1960. Social Statistics. New York: McGraw-Hill.

Bordua, D. 1961. "Delinquent Subcultures: Sociological Interpretations of Gang Delinquency." Annals of American Academy of
Political and Social Sciences 338 (November): 119-36.

Chesny-Lind, M. 1973. "Judicial Enforcement and the Female Delinquent." Issues in Criminology 8 (Fall): 51-69.

Chilton, R. J. 1964. "Continuity in Delinquency Area Research: A Comparison of Studies for Baltimore, Detroit and Indianapolis." American Sociological Review 29 (February): 71-83.

Chilton, R., and J. Dussich. 1974. "Methodological Issues in Delinquency Research: Some Alternative Analyses of Geographically Distributed Data." Social Forces 53 (September): 73-83.

Clark, J., and E. Haurek. 1966. "Age and Sex Roles of Adolescents and Their Involvement in Misconduct." Sociology and Social Research 50 (July): 496-509.

Clark, J., and L. Tifft. 1966. "Polygraph and Interview Validation of Self-Reported Deviant Behavior." American Sociological Review 31 (August): 516-23.

Clark, J., and Wenninger. 1962. "Social Class and Area as Correlates of Illegal Behavior among Juveniles." American Sociological Review 27 (December): 826-34.

Cloward, R., and L. Ohlin. 1970. "Differential Opportunity and Delinquent Subcultures." In Society, Delinquency and Delinquent Behavior, edited by H. Voss. Boston: Little, Brown.

_____. 1960. Delinquency and Opportunity: A Theory of Delinquent Gangs. New York: Free Press.

Cockburn, J. J., and I. McClay. 1965. "Sex Differentials in Juvenile Delinquency." British Journal of Criminology 5 (July): 289-309.

Cohen, A. 1955. Delinquent Boys: The Culture of the Gang. New York: Free Press.

Cohen, A., and J. Short. 1958. "Research in Delinquent Subcultures." Journal of Social Issues 14: 20-37.

Coleman, J. 1961. The Adolescent Society. New York: Free Press.

Conklin, J. 1972. Robbery and the Criminal Justice System. Philadelphia: J. B. Lippincott.

Cowie, J., V. Cowie, and E. Slater. 1968. Delinquency in Girls. London: Heineman.

Cressey, D. 1957. "The State of Criminal Statistics." National Probation and Parole Association Journal 3: 230-41.

Datesman, S., F. Scarpitti, and R. Stephenson. 1975. "Female Delinquency: An Application of Self and Opportunity Theories." Journal of Research in Crime and Delinquency 12 (July): 107-23.

David, L. 1972. "The Gentle Sex?" Today's Health, July, pp. 47-49.

Davis, K. 1937. "The Sociology of Prostitution." American Sociological Review 2 (October): 744-55.

Dentler, R. 1963. "Notes on the Self-Report Technique in the Study of Juvenile Misconduct." In Key Issues in Criminology, edited by R. Hood and R. Sparks. New York: McGraw-Hill.

Denys, R. 1969. "Lady Paperhangers." Canadian Journal of Corrections 11: 165-92.

Elliott, M. 1952. Crime in Modern Society. New York: Harper & Bros.

Empey, L. T., and M. L. Erickson. 1966. "Hidden Delinquency and Social Status." Social Forces 44 (June): 546-54.

Erickson, M. 1972. "The Changing Relationship between Official and Self-Reported Measures of Delinquency: An Exploratory Predictive Study." Journal of Criminal Law, Criminology and Police Science 63: 388-95.

Erickson, M. L., and L. T. Empey. 1963. "Court Records, Undetected Delinquency and Decision Making." Journal of Criminal Law, Criminology and Police Science 54 (December): 456-69.

Faris, R. L., ed. 1974. Handbook of Modern Sociology. Chicago: Rank McNally.

Felice, M., and D. Offord. 1972. "Three Developmental Pathways to Delinquency in Girls." British Journal of Criminology 12 (October): 375-89.

_____. 1971. "Girl Delinquency . . . A Review." Corrective Psychiatry and Journal of Social Therapy 17: 18-33.

Figlio, R. 1975. "The Seriousness of Offenses: An Evaluation by Offenders and Non Offenders." Journal of Criminal Law and Criminology 66 (June): 189-201.

Forer, L. 1970. No One Will Listen—How Our Legal System Brutalizes the Youthful Poor. New York: John Day.

Freeman, J. 1975. The Politics of Women's Liberation. New York: David McKay.

_____. 1973. "The Origins of the Women's Liberation Movement." American Journal of Sociology 78 (January): 792-811.

Freud, S. 1933. New Introductory Lectures on Psycholoanalysis. New York: W. W. Norton.

Giallombardo, R. 1974. The Social World of Imprisoned Girls. New York: John Wiley & Sons.

Gibbons, D. 1977. Society, Crime and Criminal Careers. Englewood Cliffs, N.J.: Prentice-Hall.

Gibson, H. B. 1967. "Self-Reported Delinquency among Schoolboys and Their Attitudes to the Police." British Journal of Social and Clinical Psychology 6: 168-73.

Gilbert, J. 1972. "Delinquent (Approved School) and Non Delinquent (Secondary Modern School) Girls." British Journal of Criminology, October, pp. 325-56.

Giordano, P. 1976. "Changing Sex Roles and Females' Involvement in Delinquency." Paper presented at the Annual Meeting of the Midwest Sociological Society, April, at St. Louis, Mo.

_____. 1974. "The Juvenile Justice System: The Client Perspective." Ph.D. dissertation, University of Minnesota.

Glaser, D. 1964. The Effectiveness of a Prison and Parole System. New York: Bobbs-Merrill.

Glaser, B., and A. Strauss. 1966. The Discovery of Grounded Theory. Chicago: Aldine.

Glenn, Norval. 1977. Cohort Analysis. Beverly Hills: Sage.

Glenn, N., and R. Zody. 1970. "Cohort Analysis with National Survey Data." Gerontologist 10 (Autumn): 233-40.

Glueck, S., and E. Glueck. 1934. Five Hundred Delinquent Women. New York: Alfred A. Knopf.

Gold, M. 1966. "Undetected Delinquent Behavior." Journal of Research in Crime and Delinquency 3 (January): 27-46.

Goldman, N. 1963. The Differential Selection of Juvenile Offenders for Court Appearance. New York: National Research and Information Center.

Gove, Wa. 1975. The Labeling of Deviance: Evaluating a Perspective. New York: John Wiley & Sons.

Green, E. 1970. "Race, Social Status and Criminal Arrest." American Sociological Review 35 (June): 476-90.

Hammond, P. 1969. "Aging and the Ministry." In Aging and the Professions, edited by M. Riley, J. Riley, and M. Johnson. Aging and Society, vol. 2. New York: Russell Sage Foundation.

Hansen, J. 1975. "Women's Rights and Wrongs." New York Times, March 17, p. 23.

Hardt, R., and G. Bodine. 1965. Development of Self Report Instruments in Delinquency Research. Syracuse, N.Y.: Syracuse University, Youth Development Center.

Hare, Nathan. 1970. "Black Women 1970." Transaction 8: 65-69.

Harris, A. 1977. "Sex and Theories of Deviance: Toward a Functional Theory of Deviant Type Scripts." American Sociological Review 42 (February): 3-18.

Hartjen, Clayton. 1974. Crime and Criminalization. New York: Praeger.

Hindelang, M. 1971. "Age, Sex and the Versatility of Delinquent Involvements." Social Problems 18 (Spring): 522-35.

Hirschi, T. 1969. Causes of Delinquency. Berkeley and Los Angeles: University of California Press.

Hoffman-Bustamante, D. 1973. "The Nature of Female Criminality." Issues in Criminology 8 (Fall): 117-36.

Hole, J., and E. Levine. 1971. Rebirth of Feminism. New York: Quadrangle.

Hood, R., and R. Sparks. 1970. Key Issues in Criminology. New York: McGraw-Hill.

Horowitz, R., and G. Schwartz. 1974. "Honor, Normative Ambiguity and Gang Violence." American Sociological Review 39: 238-52.

Kamarovsky, M. 1962. Blue Collar Marriage. New York: Free Press.

Klein, D. 1973. "The Etiology of Female Crime." Issues in Criminology 8 (Fall): 3-31.

Klein, M., and G. Luce. 1971. "Delinquent Girl Gangs." In U.S. National Institute of Mental Health, The Mental Health of the Child, pp. 395-97. Washington, D.C.: U.S. Government Printing Office.

Konopka, G. 1966. The Adolescent Girl in Conflict. Englewood Cliffs, N.J.: Prentice-Hall.

La Rue, L. 1970. "Black Liberation and Women's Lib." Transaction 8: 59-64.

Lander, B. 1954. Toward an Understanding of Juvenile Delinquency. New York: Columbia University Press.

Lemert, E. 1967. "The Concept of Secondary Deviation." In Human Deviance, Social Problems and Social Control, edited by E. Lemert. Englewood Cliffs, N.J.: Prentice-Hall.

Lombroso, C. 1920. The Female Offender. New York: Appleton.

Lopata, H. 1971. Occupation: Housewife. London: Oxford University Press.

McEachern, A., and R. Bauzer. 1967. "Factors Related to Disposition in Juvenile Police Contacts." In Juvenile Gangs in Context Theory, Research and Action, edited by M. W. Klein and B. G. Meyerhoff, pp. 148-60. Englewood Cliffs, N.J.: Prentice-Hall.

Mannheim, K. 1952. "The Problem of Generations." In Essays on the Sociology of Knowledge, edited and translated by Paul Kecskemeti. London: Routledge & Kegan Paul.

Merton, R. 1957. Social Theory and Social Structure. New York: Free Press.

_____. 1938. "Social Theory and Anomie." American Sociological Review 3 (October): 672-82.

Miller, W. 1973. "The Molls." Society 11 (November-December): 32-35.

_____. 1958. "Lower Class Culture as a Generating Milieu of Gang Delinquency." Journal of Social Issues 14: 5-19.

Mills, C. W. 1967. The Sociological Imagination. New York: Oxford University Press.

Morris, R. R. 1964. "Female Delinquency and Relational Problems." Social Forces 43 (October): 12-28.

Normandeau, A. 1966. "The Measurement of Delinquency in Montreal." Journal of Criminal Law, Criminology and Police Science 57 (June): 172-77.

Nye, I. 1958. Family Relationships and Delinquent Behavior. New York: Wiley.

Orback, R. 1961. "Aging and Religion: A Study of Church Attendance in the Detroit Metropolitan Area." Geriatrics 16: 530-40.

Piliavin, I., and S. Briar. 1964. "Police Encounters with Juveniles." American Journal of Sociology 70 (September): 206-14.

Pollak, O. 1950. The Criminality of Women. Philadelphia: University of Pennsylvania Press.

Pollak, D., and A. Friedman. 1969. Family Dynamics and Female Sex Delinquency. Palo Alto, Calif.: Science and Behavior Books.

Quinney, R. 1970. The Social Reality of Crime. Boston: Little, Brown.

Reckless, W. C. 1957. "Female Criminality." National Probation and Parole Association Journal 3 (January): 1-6.

Reiss, A. 1971. The Police and the Public. New Haven, Conn.: Yale University Press.

Rettig, R., M. Torres, and G. Garrett. 1977. Manny: A Criminal-Addict's Story. Boston: Houghton-Mifflin.

Riege, M. G. 1972. "Parental Affection and Juvenile Delinquency." British Journal of Criminology, January, pp. 55-73.

Riley, M., and A. Foner. 1968. An Inventory of Research Findings. Aging and Society, vol. 1. New York: Russell Sage Foundation.

Riley, M., M. Johnson, and A. Foner, eds. 1972. A Sociology of Age Stratification. Aging and Society, vol. 3. New York: Russell Sage Foundation.

Rossi, Waite, Bose, and Berk. 1974. "The Seriousness of Crimes: Normative Structure and Individual Differences." American Sociological Review 39 (April): 224-37.

Ryder, N. 1972. "Notes on the Concept of Population." In A Sociology of Age Stratification, edited by M. Riley, M. Johnson, and A. Foner. Aging and Society, vol. 3. New York: Russell Sage Foundation.

_____. "The Cohort as a Concept in the Study of Social Change." American Sociological Review 30 (December): 843-61.

_____. "Notes on the Concept of a Population." American Journal of Sociology 69 (December): 447-63.

Sainsbury, P. 1963. "Social and Epidemiological Aspects of Suicide with Special Reference to Aged." In Process of Aging, edited by R. Williams, C. Tibbitts, and W. Donahue, vol. 2. New York: Atherton Press.

Schaie, K. 1965. "A General Model for the Study of Developmental Problems." Psychological Bulletin 64: 92-107.

Sellin, T. 1951. "The Significance of Records of Crime." Law Quarterly Review 67 (October): 489-504.

Sellin, T., and M. Wolfgang. 1964. The Measurement of Delinquency. New York: John Wiley & Sons.

Shaw, H., and D. McKay. 1942. Juvenile Delinquency in Urban Areas. Chicago: University of Chicago Press.

Short, J. 1968. Gang Delinquency and Delinquent Subculture. New York: Harper & Row.

Short, J. F., and I. Nye. 1970. "Extent of Unrecorded Juvenile Delinquency: Tentative Conclusion." In Juvenile Delinquency: A Reader, edited by N. Teele, pp. 10-16. Itasca, Ill.: Peacock.

_____. 1958. "Extent of Unrecorded Juvenile Delinquency." Journal of Criminal Law, Criminology and Police Science 49 (November-December): 296-302.

Short, J. F., and F. Strodtbeck. 1965. Group Process and Gang Delinquency. Chicago: University of Chicago Press.

Simon, R. 1975. The Contemporary Woman and Crime. Rockville, Md.: National Institute of Mental Health, Crime and Delinquency Issues.

Smith, A. 1962. Women in Prison. London: Stevens & Sons.

Smith, H. M. S. 1975. Strategies of Social Research. Englewood Cliffs, N.J.: Prentice-Hall.

Staples, R. 1971. "Toward a Sociology of Black Female: A Theoretical and Methodological Assessment." Journal of Marriage and Family, February, pp. 119-35.

Stouffer, S. 1955. Communism, Conformity and Civil Liberties. Garden City, N.Y.: Doubleday.

Sutherland, E. 1939. Principles of Criminology. 3d ed. Philadelphia: J. B. Lippincott.

Sutherland, E., and D. Cressey. 1978. Criminology. 10th ed. New York: J. B. Lippincott.

_____. 1970. Criminology. 8th ed. Philadelphia: J. B. Lippincott.

Suttles, G. 1968. The Social Order of the Slum. Chicago: University of Chicago Press.

Terry, R. 1967. "Discrimination in the Handling of Juvenile Offenders by Social Control Agencies." Journal of Research in Crime and Delinquency 4 (July): 219-30.

Thomas, P. 1967. Down These Mean Streets. New York: New American Library.

Thomas, W. I. 1923. The Unadjusted Girl. Boston: Little, Brown.

_____. 1907. Sex and Society. Boston: Little, Brown.

Thornberry, T. 1973. "Race, Socioeconomic Status and Sentencing in the Juvenile Justice System." Journal of Criminal Law and Criminology 64 (March): 90-98.

Toby, J. 1957. "Differential Impact of Family Disorganization." American Sociological Review 22 (October): 505-12.

U.S., Department of Commerce, Bureau of the Census. 1977. Statistical Abstracts. Washington, D.C.: Government Printing Office.

U.S., Department of Justice, Federal Bureau of Investigation. 1975. Uniform Crime Reports. Washington, D.C.: Government Printing Office.

_____. 1971. U.S. Reporting Handbook: How to Prepare Uniform Crime Reports. Washington, D.C.: Government Printing Office.

_____. 1966. U.S. Reporting Handbook: How to Prepare Uniform Crime Reports. Washington, D.C.: Government Printing Office.

_____. 1964. U.S. Reporting Handbook: How to Prepare Uniform Crime Reports. Washington, D.C.: Government Printing Office.

_____. 1962. U.S. Reporting Handbook: How to Prepare Uniform Crime Reports. Washington, D.C.: Government Printing Office.

_____. 1955. U.S. Reporting Handbook: How to Prepare Uniform Crime Reports. Washington, D.C.: Government Printing Office.

_____. 1949. U.S. Reporting Handbook: How to Prepare Uniform Crime Reports. Washington, D.C.: Government Printing Office.

U.S., President's Commission on Law Enforcement and Administration of Justice, Task Force Report. 1967. "Economic Factors on Delinquency." Appendix O., Juvenile Delinquency and Youth Crime. Washington, D.C.: Government Printing Office, pp. 305-16.

Vaz, E. 1966. "Self Reported Delinquency and Socio-Economic Status." Canadian Journal of Corrections 8: 20-27.

Vedder, C. 1954. The Juvenile Offender. New York: Doubleday.

Vedder, C., and D. Somerville. 1970. The Delinquent Girl. Springfield, Ill.: Charles Thomas.

Ward, J. 1969. "Crimes of Violence by Women." In Crimes of Violence: A Staff Report Submitted to the National Commission on the Causes and Prevention of Violence, vol. 3. Washington, D.C.: U.S. Government Printing Office, app. 17: 843-907.

Wattenberg, W. 1957. "Girl Repeaters." National Probation and Parole Association Journal 3 (January): 48-54.

Weis, J. 1976. "Liberation and Crime: The Invention of the New Female Criminal." Paper presented at Pacific Sociological Association Meeting, March 27, San Diego.

Wellford, C., and M. Wiatrowski. 1975. "On the Measurement of Delinquency." Journal of Criminal Law and Criminology 66 (June): 175-89.

Whyte, W. F. 1955. Street Corner Society. Chicago: University of Chicago Press.

Wise, N. B. 1967. "Juvenile Delinquency among Middle Class Girls." In Middle Class Juvenile Delinquency, edited by E. W. Vaz, pp. 179-88. New York: Harper & Row.

Wolfgang, M. 1963. "Uniform Crime Reports: A Critical Appraisal." University of Pennsylvania Law Review 111: 708-35.

Wolfgang, M., R. Figlio, and T. Sellin. 1972. Delinquency in a Birth Cohort. Chicago: University of Chicago Press.

Yablonsky, L. 1967. The Violent Gang. Baltimore: Penguin Books.

INDEX

Adler, Freda, 12–13
adult arrests: male-female comparison of, 68–71; rates of male and female, 39–40; same-sex comparison of, 66–71
age: chronological, 94–95; controlling for, 66–71; effects of, 101–3; at first offense, 77–78, 80; and frequency of offense, 66–71 (see also aging)
aggressiveness, 112
aging, 23, 84–86, 88, 89–90 (see also age)
antiwar movement, 82, 83
arrest: figures, increases in, 14; files, 28–29; records, 21, 22, 23, 24, 25; reports, 21–24 [adult, information contained on, 29–30]; statistics, 61–62, 66 (see also arrest rate; arrests)
arrest rate: changes in, 34–35; changing, 13; and demographic changes, 35; difference in, between males and females, 10; female, 11, 104–5; impact of women's movement on, 104–6; increases in, 17–18, 52; index of, 37, 41, 48; national, for males and females, 34; per thousand, 49–51; for women, 1, 2, 5
arrests: change in rate of, for juveniles and adults, 37–48, 49–50; female, 14, 37–41, 52, 57–58; increase in, 14, 35–48, 49–51, 58, 60; of juveniles and adults, 51; versus offenders, 51–52; percentage of, rise in, 56; rise in, 112, 113 [by race

and social class, 56–57]; seriousness of [and age, 67, 68; increased, 67, 114; and race, 61; and sex, 58–60; and social class, 60–61]; per thousand population, 49–51
arson, 18 n
assault, 13, 60, 81, 105; aggravated, 18 n, 60; on police, 61, 81; simple, 60, 61
auto theft, 18 n, 48

behavior utility (see utility, behavior)
biological differences among boys and girls, 6–7
biological factors for crime, 5
blackmail, 108
burglary, 18 n, 34, 48, 109

civil rights demonstrations, 16
cohort: analysis, 15, 23, 28, 31, 84–103, 113 [of trends in crime severity, 84–89]; diagonal, 85, 88; differences, 84–86, 89, 94–95, 103, 114 [by age and sex, 89–95]; effects, 23, 88, 99, 103; flow, 84, 89; patterns for males and females, 89–96; studies, 24
cohorts: baby-boom, 100; birth, 23, 84, 89, 90; composition of, 88–89; demographic characteristics of, 99, 114; life cycle of, 85–86; same-age, 15, 95; same-sex, 94–95; selection of, for research, 24–28; sequential, 84; seriousness of offense of, 89–90; single, 86; standard table of, 85

ABOUT THE AUTHOR

JOANN GENNARO GORA is an Assistant Professor of Sociology at Fairleigh Dickinson University in Madison, New Jersey. In addition to her academic position, she received an American Council of Education fellowship to study and do research on academic administration.

Dr. Gora has done extensive research in the area of criminology and organizational behavior. She has received a U.S. Department of Health and Human Services research grant to study volunteerism in the medical sector.

Dr. Gora holds a B.A. from Vassar College and an M.A. and Ph.D. from Rutgers University.